MEETING JESUS ON THE ROAD TO EMMAUS

MEETING
JESUS
on the ROAD
to EMMAUS

An Invitation to Friendship, Eucharist
and Christian Community

DENNIS J. BILLY C.SS.R.

TWENTY-THIRD
PUBLICATIONS

twentythirdpublications.com

IN LOVING MEMORY OF

Walter and Helene Sullivan

Cover art: ©Superstock / akg-images

TWENTY-THIRD PUBLICATIONS
One Montauk Avenue, Suite 200
New London, CT 06320
(860) 437-3012 or (800) 321-0411
www.twentythirdpublications.com

ISBN: 978-1-62785-326-2
Library of Congress Control Number: 2017945080
Printed in the U.S.A.

 A Division of Bayard, Inc.

CONTENTS

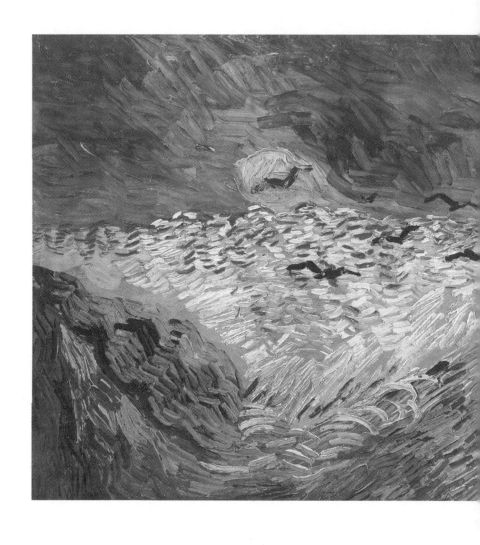

*Then they told what had happened
on the road, and how he had been made known
to them in the breaking of the bread.*

LUKE 24:35

INTRODUCTION

The story in Luke's gospel of the two disciples' encounter with the Risen Lord on the road to Emmaus (Luke 24:13–35) contains many lessons about the journey of faith and what it means to be a follower of Christ. It is one of the most intriguing of Jesus' resurrection appearances, since Christians can identify closely with these disciples and, in many ways, claim their experience for themselves. We are all called to follow in the Lord's footsteps.

Jesus once said, "If any want to become my followers, let them deny themselves and take up their cross daily and follow me" (Luke 9:23).[1] This call comes from Jesus himself, who since the day of his resurrection has manifested himself to his disciples in any number of ways. In the Emmaus story, he reveals himself to them by conversing with them, explaining the Scriptures to them, befriending them, breaking bread with them, and sending them back into community. To this day, Jesus continues to show himself to his followers. What happened to the two disciples on the road to Emmaus happens to everyone who walks by the light of faith and allows it to motivate their lives and influence their actions in daily life.

This book traces the journey of these two disciples and translates that experience for today's disciples. Each of its six chapters has something significant to say about the life of discipleship. Chapter One, "The Road to Emmaus," looks at Luke's account as it would have been understood by the Christians of his day and goes on to make relevant adaptations for today's believers. Chapter Two, "Called to Prayer," focuses on the ways we can converse with Jesus in our journey through life and emphasizes the importance of praying to God on every level of our being. Chapter Three, "Searching the Scriptures," places Jesus at the heart of biblical interpretation and says that the primary purpose of Holy Writ is to reveal the face of God. Chapter Four, "Our Befriending Lord," recognizes that Jesus not only accompanies us on the road, but also befriends us on our journey and enters into a personal relationship with each of us. Chapter Five, "In the Breaking of the Bread," emphasizes Jesus' presence in Christian table fellowship and how he reveals himself to his disciples especially in every eucharistic gathering. The final chapter, "Called to Community," locates the call to discipleship in the heart of the body of believers and recognizes that it is from there that the proclamation of the gospel extends to all the corners of the earth. A series of reflection questions under the heading "On the Road to Emmaus" appears at the end of each chapter to assist us in appropriating the Emmaus narrative and finding its specific relevance for our lives. Each chapter concludes with a prayer to Jesus, "My Burning Heart," that invites him to accompany us at every stage of the faith journey and asks him for help in responding to his call to discipleship.

Luke's account of the two disciples on the road to Emmaus has great relevance for us today. It teaches us that the gospel receives its power in an encounter with the Risen Lord, who reveals himself to us in many ways and uses us to reach out to others. The spread of the gospel flows from this authentic encounter and cannot be sustained without it. This encounter often takes place while we are on the road and at times when we do not clearly recognize Jesus' presence in our midst. For this reason, the story of Emmaus is also our story. It teaches us that Jesus' disciples follow him because they love him with a love that opens their eyes and enables them to see him in their midst through the eyes of faith and to continue their journey with renewed hope and confidence of his abiding presence. May this book help you in your journey of faith. May it deepen your love for the Lord and renew your hope in the coming of his kingdom. May it help you recognize him in your midst and, most especially, in the breaking of the bread.

CHAPTER ONE

The ROAD *to* EMMAUS

The story in Luke's gospel of the two disciples on the road to Emmaus expresses the soul of the Christian message and resonates deeply in the hearts of the faithful. It does so, because it serves as a bridge between the Risen Lord's appearances to his disciples and that of the believing community's experience of him in the Scriptures and the breaking of the bread. Its significance stems from its position in Luke's gospel and its powerful claim that the Risen Lord accompanies his followers in their journey of faith. Down through the ages, Christians have found themselves reflected in this story of the encounter of these two disciples with their Lord. They see themselves on a similar journey. Like the two disciples, they know that the call to follow Christ, once freely embraced, will change their lives forever.

Some Background

Jesus' appearance to two disciples as they were walking on the road actually occurs twice in the gospels: once in Mark 16:12–13 and again in Luke 24:13–35. Mark's rendering is by far the shortest: "After this he appeared in another form to two of them, as they were walking into the country. And they went back and told the rest, but they did not believe them." Luke offers many more details and makes the encounter a central feature in his gospel.

The two accounts differ not only in length, but also in some key points. A few verses earlier, Mark's account says that Jesus appeared to Mary Magdalene, but that no one believed her (Mark 16:9–11), just as no one believed the two disciples when they recounted their experience. Luke's account, by way of contrast, suggests that the two disciples were greeted with joy and excitement upon returning to Jerusalem and that they themselves received the news that Jesus had appeared to Simon (Luke 24:34). Such discrepancies probably stem from subtle variances in the eyewitness accounts themselves and from the particular themes that

Luke wished to emphasize in his gospel. His telling of Jesus' appearance to the two disciples on the road to Emmaus touches many points of the gospel message and teems with significance for the faith.

Luke's gospel roughly dates from about 85 AD, some fifty years after Jesus' death and resurrection.[2] By this time the nascent church had expanded throughout much of the Roman world and made great progress in evangelizing the Gentile nations. Luke addresses a largely Gentile Christian audience and shapes his message toward issues that directly impact their lives, not the least of which were questions about the nearness of the end times and the Lord's Second Coming. By now, already a couple of generations removed from Jesus' post-resurrection appearances, Luke's readers are wondering about the Lord's immanent return, a conviction so much in the foreground of the early Christian message.

The burning questions in the hearts of his audience concern the authenticity of their own faith experience and its continuity with the Risen Lord's appearances to his early disciples. What are they to do if the Risen Lord has ascended to the right hand of the Father yet his return is no longer considered immanent? Has the Lord left them to fend for themselves in their historical journey? How are they to experience him in their present reality? Luke's response to these concerns is that the faithful must now rely on the ongoing presence of the Lord's Spirit in the believing community, especially as he reveals himself through the Scriptures and in the breaking of the bread. The account of the two disciples on the road to

Emmaus addresses these concerns and speaks on a number of levels to the experience of these second- and third-generation Gentile Christians.

The Emmaus Story (Luke 24:13–35)

Unlike the other gospels, Luke presents the Emmaus encounter as Jesus' first post-resurrection appearance. As the story unfolds, two disciples are making their way from Jerusalem to the nearby village of Emmaus, some three days after Jesus' death and burial. As they walk along, discussing the events of recent days, Jesus draws near to them and asks them what they are discussing. Looking downcast and prevented from recognizing him, they stop in their tracks and ask him if he is the only one in Jerusalem who has not heard of the things that have happened to Jesus of Nazareth, about his suffering and death, the empty tomb, and the claim by some of the women that angels had announced to them that he was alive. After reprimanding these disciples for their foolishness and slowness of heart, Jesus opens the Scriptures up to them, explaining everything in Moses and the prophets about the suffering the Messiah must undergo in order to enter into his glory. Later in their journey, as they reach the village and with evening drawing near, the two disciples convince Jesus to stay with them. Later on, while they are at table, he takes bread, says the blessing, and breaks it. At that moment, their eyes are opened, they recognize him as their Master, and he just as quickly vanishes from their midst. Overwhelmed with joy, the two set out immediately for Jerusalem to tell the other disciples about what they have experienced. They, in turn, are greeted with the news that Jesus has indeed risen and has appeared to Simon.

Luke places this gospel story in a strategic location in his gospel. Prior to it, he tells of the discovery of the empty tomb by some of the women, a simple announcement by two men in dazzling clothes that Jesus is risen, and the unbelief with which the discovery of the women was met (Luke 24:1–12). Afterward, when the two disciples return to Jerusalem to share what had happened to them, the disciples in Jerusalem confirm their experience by announcing that Jesus has risen and has appeared to Simon. Then, at that very moment, Jesus himself appears in their midst, greets them, shows them his wounds, asks them for something to eat, opens up the Scriptures to them, tells them to be witnesses of his resurrection, promises to send his Spirit, blesses them, and is then carried up to heaven (Luke 24:36–52). The implication is clear. The story of the two disciples on the road to Emmaus is a central feature of the Easter proclamation. Luke integrates the experience of the two disciples in an intimate way with the Easter event. He accentuates its importance by recounting it first and, in doing so, placing it on the same level as the discovery of the empty tomb and Jesus' appearance to Simon.

Luke's audience could identify closely with the two disciples who encounter Jesus on the road. Other than their mention in this story, these disciples are unknown to the rest of the New Testament. Although one is identified as Cleopas, nothing else is known of him and, for all practical purposes, he remains as faceless as his traveling companion. This anonymity is one of the strengths of the story, since down through the ages most of the Christian faithful have themselves left few historical markers behind with the result that their identities also remain clouded in the fog of history. This lack of detail raises a number of questions and invites Christians to engage the story with their imaginations. Why do these two disciples seem in such a rush to leave Jerusalem so soon after the death of their Master? Why are they traveling together? Is the unnamed disciple male or female? What is the precise nature of their relationship? Why are they traveling to Emmaus? Where exactly *is* this village? Its very existence would have been lost to history were it not for its mention in this gospel story. Luke's readers could easily place themselves in the sandals of the two disciples making their way to this unknown country village. When reading the story, moreover, they could easily be led to ask themselves how Jesus might appear to them as they make their way in their walk of faith and if they too would be able to recognize him as he joins them on the road of life, in the Scriptures, and in the breaking of the bread.

The Journey of Faith

In this way, Luke's account of the two disciples who encounter Jesus on the road to Emmaus has embedded itself in the Christian imagination. Christians who read this story and ponder it understand that it is very much about their own journey of faith. In one way or another, each of us is on the road to Emmaus. The story unfolds in a way that resonates in the heart of every disciple. It is a story of disillusionment, encounter, discovery, and joy. This story of faith has left an impression on our minds that cannot and will not soon be forgotten.

Luke casts his story in the context of a journey, a theme that permeates much of his gospel narrative and that has clear implications for the life of discipleship. As Jesus' journey to Jerusalem covers the central chapters of Luke's gospel narrative (Luke 9:51–19:27), so the journey of the two disciples away from and then back to Jerusalem marks a central feature of the Good News as it unfolds in the life of every believer. Jesus goes to Jerusalem to suffer death and rise to fulfill his Father's will. The two disciples return to Jerusalem because they have experienced the Risen Lord and wish to share that news with the community of disciples they left behind. The faith of every believer has its roots in this Easter experience. The Christ event—Jesus' passion, death, and resurrection— takes place in Jerusalem, and it is from there that the gospel message will take shape and first be proclaimed.

In addition to the theme of journey, the story also stands out because so little is known about the village of Emmaus itself, making it, in effect, a destination that could be virtually anywhere in the minds of the faithful. Although several locations have been suggested, scholars have struggled to identify the village's exact whereabouts.[3] Since the two disciples were making their way there by foot, it was most likely within a day's walk from Jerusalem and accessible by road. These scant details, while limiting for the historian, leave us free to imagine ourselves on a similar journey. Moreover, that *two* disciples were traveling together to this small village brings to mind the mission of the seventy disciples, whom Jesus sent out in pairs to the neighboring towns and villages that he himself was planning to visit (Luke 10:1–16). Could it be that these two disciples numbered among the seventy and that Emmaus was one of the villages visited by them when they were on their mission? Could it also be that they were returning to Emmaus to share the news of the recent events with the people there? What was their business there? Did they come from there? Did they have friends and family there? Were they going there to warn others? Were they fleeing? Were they going there to hide? Although the precise reason for the disciples traveling to Emmaus so soon after Jesus' death and burial will never be known with certainty, it is not improbable that fear, despondency, and perhaps even disillusionment played at least a small role in their motivation for leaving Jerusalem at such a crucial time. Just as significant was their great joy in experiencing Jesus in the breaking of the bread, and the eucharistic overtones this would have for the readers of Luke's gospel.

Encountering Christ

The Emmaus story is about the personal encounter that two downcast, possibly disillusioned, disciples have with the Risen Lord. In the course of this encounter, Jesus conceals his identity as he accompanies them. After he converses with them, opens up the Scriptures to them, breaks bread with them, and finally reveals himself to them, he suddenly vanishes from their sight. As the story unfolds, their somber and downcast mood gives way to a sense of urgency and sends them running back to Jerusalem to share the Good News of the Lord's resurrection. After their experience of Jesus on the road, everything changes. Nothing remains the same. They now have a message to share, Good News to tell. Their entire focus is now on proclaiming the gospel message. All else is secondary.

This story captures the joy of experiencing the Risen Lord. In it, Luke reminds his readers that the same Christ whom the two disciples encounter on the road to Emmaus accompanies all believers in their journey of faith. He affirms that Christ reveals himself in a special way whenever they converse with him in prayer, ponder the Scriptures, befriend a stranger on the way, break bread together, and live in community. Although they may not always recognize him as they carry out these basic tasks of Christian discipleship, he is there nonetheless and promises to give them a genuine, if not fleeting, sense of his ongoing and steadfast presence.

From beginning to end, this story is about the walk of discipleship. It challenges us to delve more deeply into the various practices that support us in our journey of faith and asks us to discern if they mediate a personal encounter with the Risen Lord or have become nothing but empty structures that fail to impart life. It invites us to examine our lives and ask ourselves if we believe that Jesus accompanies us in our journey of faith and if we believe he is really listening to us when we pray. It asks us to look at our expectations about experiencing him in the Scriptures, in our celebration of Eucharist, and in our life together. It reminds us that such practices—prayer, friendship, discernment, meditating on Scripture, Eucharist, and community—are central to the intimate encounter with Christ in a person's life and to the life of discipleship. It affirms what every Christian seeks and yearns for. It reminds us that the Christ of faith is one with the Jesus of history and can be experienced by anyone who is led by the light of faith and who opens their heart to the fire of his love.

Life in Christ

The Emmaus story also focuses on gospel living. The experience of the two disciples changed their entire outlook on life and instilled in them a desire to follow Christ and share in his life and work. Their motivation for doing so stemmed from their firsthand experience of the Risen Lord. When they recognized him in the breaking of the bread they understood how he had accompanied them on the road, conversed with them, and unfolded the meaning of the Scriptures to them. They understood that Christ was present to them not only when they were at table, but also during the in-between places of life: when meeting a stranger on the road, in their conversation on the way, when showing hospitality at the end of journey. The early Christian community would take this message to heart by seeing that the gospel message was meant to permeate all of life.

The implications of this insight are clear. When Jesus opened up the Scriptures to the two disciples and explained to them that it was necessary for the Messiah to suffer so that he could enter into his glory, he was inviting them to probe the Scriptures still further and to see their own lives reflected in his paschal mystery. In interpreting this passage, the early Christian community would come to see that in this passage Jesus was referring not only to the suffering that he himself had recently undergone, but also to the suffering that lay ahead for his followers. Luke's readers would see that the Risen Lord encountered by the two disciples on the road to Emmaus was the same as the one they celebrated whenever they gathered for Eucharist. To break bread together was a celebration of their intimate communion with his Body and Blood and, hence, his suffering, death, and resurrection.

During his life on earth, Jesus had said repeatedly that anyone wishing to be his disciple must take up his cross and follow him. Only by following him in this way could they share in his glory. The two disciples return to Jerusalem when they recognize him in the breaking of the bread, because they know that his resurrection confirmed everything that he ever said and did. In one way or another, we are all called to return to Jerusalem in order to announce the good news and continue the work of Christ's redeeming love. To encounter the Risen Lord—be it at the empty tomb in Jerusalem, on the road to Emmaus, or wherever Christians gather to break bread together—means living in communion with him and sharing that communion with others in mission.

Conclusion

The Emmaus story touches our hearts because it speaks to our experience. Christians generations (and now centuries) removed from the apostles' experience of the Risen Lord can relate to this tale of the two disciples' encounter with the Risen Lord in the breaking of the bread and see his presence reflected in their own celebration of Eucharist. All that is necessary is to view this celebration through the eyes of faith— "for we walk by faith," as the apostle Paul reminds us, "not by sight" (2 Corinthians 5:7). The story of the two disciples on the road to Emmaus challenges us to walk by faith. It invites us to delve beneath appearances of things and to experience Christ's gentle, unassuming presence with us at every step in our journey through life. It stresses the continuity between the earthly, historical Jesus, the Risen Lord, and his presence in the eucharistic celebration. That continuity lies at the very heart of the proclamation of the faith and Jesus' promise that he would be with his disciples always, even until the end of time.

Although the Emmaus story occurs at the end of Luke's gospel, it is important to remember that the gospel's sequel, the Acts of the Apostles, was authored by the same hand and intended to recount the early missionary activity of the apostles as they proclaimed the gospel message in the power of the Holy Spirit and took Christ's missionary journey from Jerusalem to the Gentile world.[4] When seen in this light, the Emmaus story, with its strong eucharistic overtones, represents a narrative hinge that unites the two volumes. In a way, the two narratives are made one in the breaking of the bread: the two disciples returned to Jerusalem after recognizing Jesus in the breaking of the bread (Luke 24:35); the early community of disciples devoted themselves to the instruction of the apostles, the communal life, the breaking of the bread, and the prayers (Acts 2:42). The implication is clear. For Luke, the Eucharist lies at the heart of the church and was one of its central features both before and after the Pentecost event. The breaking of the bread, in other words, keeps the Christian community in touch with the Risen Lord and the power of his Spirit.

In the end, the Emmaus story is all about the call to discipleship. The same Christ who encountered the two disciples on the road is the same Christ whose Spirit accompanied Peter, Paul, and a host of other disciples in their missionary journeys, and the same Christ who walks with us as Christians seek to carry on his mission in today's world. The story reminds us that following Christ is a walk of faith, yes, but a walk that has Christ by our side and the gift of his Spirit burning in our hearts as we celebrate his presence in the breaking of the bread.

ON THE ROAD TO EMMAUS

- Have you ever been overwhelmed by events that have shattered your expectations?
- Have you ever wondered why Jesus has not come back after all this time?
- How have you experienced him in your life?
- Have you ever looked for Jesus in the Scriptures?
- Have you ever looked for him in the face of a stranger?
- Have you ever received a glimpse of him in the breaking of the bread?
- Have you ever sought him in community?

MY BURNING HEART

Lord, sometimes the circumstances of life weigh me down and I find it difficult to recognize or even sense your presence in my life. At such times, help me to trust that you are with me in the midst of my struggles and walking beside me in my journey. Deepen my faith, Lord. Help me to look for you, especially in the face of the stranger. I love you, Lord. Help me to love you more.

CHAPTER TWO

CALLED *to* PRAYER

The way of discipleship involves a series of concrete steps, the first of which involves learning how to pray. As the two disciples set out on the road to Emmaus, discussing among themselves the events of recent days, Jesus draws near to them, walks alongside them, and engages them in conversation. Christian prayer rests on a belief in a personal God who is interested in our lives and wishes to enter into relationship with us through dialogue. It involves speaking to God and listening to him. This back-and-forth movement means raising our hearts and minds to God and waiting for a response in the stillness and solitude that follows.

If silence is the language of God, an assertion attested to by saintly men and women down through the centuries, then Christians need to listen to this silence, befriend it, and ultimately make peace with it. The conversation between Jesus and the two disciples on the road to Emmaus epitomizes the call to prayer. As they walked with Jesus along the road, many words were exchanged, to be sure, but there were also many moments of unrecorded silence. These moments formed an integral part of the conversation, and were probably responsible for those times when the disciples felt their hearts burning within them.

Prayer is essential to the life of discipleship, for it touches our hearts and sustains us for the long journey ahead. With it, we have hope of reaching our destination. Without it, we can easily get distracted along the road, lose heart, depart from the proper path, and wander about aimlessly without direction or purpose.

Conversing with Jesus

The account itself says that the two disciples are discussing the events of recent days as they make their way from Jerusalem to the village of Emmaus when Jesus draws near, apparently in a disguised form since they do not recognize him. Since this stranger is going in the same direction, he decides to walk with them and join in their conversation. The two disciples obviously agree. On one level, these simple statements are nothing but the opening details of a simple narrative of three people meeting on the road and forming a small group of traveling companions. Such encounters are not at all unusual, even in today's world, and the two disciples welcome the company of this stranger, knowing that there is a certain safety in numbers as a way of anticipating the unforeseen hazards of the road.

On a deeper level, however, these details reveal a great deal about the purpose and nature of Christian prayer. To begin with, they remind us that prayer is conversational in that it involves a back-and-forth communication between God and us. For Christians, God is not a distant, impersonal force, but a person who wishes to enter into relationship with his creation. Prayer is one of the primary means by which he establishes and maintains that relationship with us. The story tells us that Jesus draws near to the two disciples as they are discussing among themselves the events of recent days and trying to make sense of all that had happened. One senses from the circumstances that they are most likely leaving Jerusalem in a state of despondency, because their hopes in him had been shattered by his recent death and burial.

Because of their love for him, however, they have found a space within their hearts that has remained open to his presence in their midst. Jesus coming to them in the form of a stranger affirms their capacity to welcome the unknown. As a result, their conversation with one another soon turns into a conversation with Jesus and, unknown to them, forms the foundation of a new, transformed relationship with their master, one that will enable them to recognize him in a variety of contexts. The story affirms that the hidden God—the God of Abraham, Isaac, and Jacob—who has revealed himself in the life of Jesus of Nazareth, continues to reveal himself beyond the passion, death, and burial of his Beloved Son. Because of the empty tomb, the Risen Lord now reveals himself in a number of hidden forms: in the face of a stranger, in the words of Scripture, in the breaking of the bread, and wherever two or three are gathered in his name. God also reveals himself in the conversations we have with his Son along the way on every level of our existence. These conversations touch the very heart of prayer and require further comment.

Our Human Makeup

To understand the overall Catholic teaching on prayer, we first need to say something about our general human makeup. All in all, we need to address four specific areas that make us who and what we are: the physical, the mental, the spiritual, and the social. A suitable starting point for the discussion of the various levels of prayer and their connection with theology is the apostle Paul's tripartite division of the human person into spirit, soul, and body:

> May the God of peace himself sanctify you entirely;
> and may your spirit and soul and body be kept sound
> and blameless at the coming of our Lord Jesus Christ.
> ■ 1 THESSALONIANS 5:23

"Body" (*soma*), for Paul, refers to corporeal human existence, not in any denigrated sense, but as a neutral, albeit essential, element of human existence. It is that part of the person that, although under the sway of "law of the flesh" (*sarx*), has been, is, and will be redeemed by those living in the Spirit of Christ. Prayer seeks expression even on this, the most visible and concrete of all levels of human existence: through vocal expression (e.g., singing, verbal meditations), symbols (e.g., the sign of the cross, uplifted arms, the holding of hands) and posture (e.g., kneeling, standing, bowing one's head), and the rigors of corporeal sacrifice (e.g., fast and abstinence). A theology of prayer that overlooks, disdains, or overly spiritualizes this very important aspect of human existence must beware of the charge of Cartesian minimalism, which reduces the body to the level of a mere machine and identifies the human person with its inside inhabiting "ghost."[5]

"Soul" (*psyche*), for Paul, refers to the conscious, affective, and deliberative level of human existence. Here, reason plays an active role in constructing the concepts upon which a positive theology of God is based. This is the level of human existence that speaks to God through the images of mental prayer. Expressions of love and affection, the examination of conscience, resolutions to action, prayers of petition, and the meditative reading of Scripture all find a place within this important constituent aspect of the human person. Here is the appropriate place for the classical understanding of theology as a science that proceeds not from self-evident principles but from the principles of divinely revealed truths. On this level, prayer supports the pursuit of theological knowledge but does not participate explicitly in its ongoing rational explication.[6]

"Spirit" (*pneuma*), for Paul, stands for the innermost depths of the human person as it is open to the divine presence and awake to God's Spirit. It is that part of the person that communes with God beneath the sphere of human consciousness and cries out, "Abba! Father!" from the depths of the human heart (Romans 8:15). In the Christian tradition, this is the level of human existence that yearns for the direct experience of God in contemplative prayer. It is that part of the human person that seeks to pierce through the theologian's conceptual constructs of the nature of the Godhead and to encounter the ultimate ground of reality as it is. Since life "in the Spirit" represents the ultimate goal of human existence, one finds here the important role in the life of the church of mystical theology, i.e., theological reflection on the nature of the human experience of the divine.[7]

As developed above, Paul's anthropology and its implications for the relationship among the various forms of prayer should also be considered in conjunction with his understanding of the church as "the body of Christ" (1 Corinthians 12:12; Ephesians 1:23; Colossians 1:18). Borrowed in part from the Platonic parallel of the human soul as "writ large" in the fabric of human society, the tripartite Pauline division translates into the Spirit, Christ as the head of the church, and the faithful who form the members of his body. Here, the social dimension of the Pauline anthropology comes to the fore, doing so in a way that highlights the fundamental communal orientation of each level of human existence. That is to say that the contemplative, mental, and physical levels of human prayer reach their fullest expression only to the extent that they are done "in Christ" and, hence, in solidarity with all those who, in varying degrees, are incorporated into his body, the church. Indeed, the fullest expression of the human person at prayer is that of the community of the church gathered around the table of the Lord. The contemplative, mental, corporeal, and social aspects of human existence come together at the precise moment when the church and its members are most fully themselves in the presence of their God.

The point being made in the above presentation is that all of the various levels of prayer in the church's tradition are *necessary* for human existence. Contemplation is not to be pitted against mental prayer; nor the latter against fast and abstinence, or against liturgical prayer. Because the human person is a complex, multidimensional reality, all of these forms are necessary to orient a particular aspect of the human person toward the transcendent ground of his or her being. That is not to say that a person may not be more disposed to one form than another, but only that all four levels—the spiritual, the mental, the corporeal, and the social—are necessary if he or she wishes to orient the entire self toward God. And because this process takes place within the lived experience of Christian community, each of these forms has a special role to play in the church's liturgical prayer. This explains the importance of singing, concrete symbols, gesture, silence, imagery, and preaching in the church's communal celebrations. From this perspective, the key question in the discussion of the types of prayer is not, "Which one level is appropriate for me at this moment in my own spiritual growth?" but "What is the proper balance to strike among all four, both within myself and within the community to which I belong?" The question, in other words, has moved from the area of personal choice to that of the proper dynamics of personal and communal prayer. What is more, I must look not only to that type of prayer to which I feel most drawn, but also that which I find most difficult and challenging. How, in others, words, am I being asked to grow in my life of prayer?

Paul makes it clear that we are not isolated individuals but social beings with material, bodily needs, an interior life of thoughts and feelings, and deep yearnings for transcendence that point us in the direction of the beyond. In his mind, we are complex, multidimensional beings who relate to one another and to God on a variety of levels. This multifaceted understanding of human existence has important implications for the way we pray. Authentic prayer presupposes faith, and therefore requires our cooperation with God's grace. We are asked to respond to this grace not merely with our minds and wills, but with everything that makes us what we are. Both the Old and New Testaments state very clearly that we must love God with our entire being: "You shall love the Lord your God with all your heart, and with all your soul, and with all your mind" (Matthew 22:37; see Deuteronomy 6:5). Since praying to God is one of the primary ways that we express our love for him, it is important for us relate to him with our bodies, our thoughts and emotions, our spirits, and as a believing community.

The Ways of Prayer

Each of these dimensions—the physical, mental, spiritual, and social—involves a particular kind of prayer, what the church calls *oratio* (vocal prayer), *meditatio* (mental prayer), *contemplatio* (contemplation), and *liturgia* (liturgy).[8] A quick look at each of these ways of praying will help us understand and appreciate the important place of prayer in our lives.

Oratio, or vocal prayer, is what we say every day and what we are probably most familiar with. It uses the voice and, by extension, other means of bodily expression to converse with God. We speak to God through the spoken word, gestures, images, incense, lighted candles—anything that engages our physical senses. We pray in this way to express our thoughts and feelings to him, seek his guidance, and articulate our needs. This is how we first learn to speak to God, and we continually return to it. The Sign of the Cross, the Hail Mary, the Our Father, and Morning Offering are all prayers that many of us learned as children and return to again and again in our adult lives. Vocal prayer can be prayed either individually or in groups. Although it often relies on set formulas, it can also involve spontaneous outpourings of the heart.[9]

Meditatio, or mental prayer, goes on in our minds and focuses primarily on thought, imagination, memory, and feelings. We still use words to talk with God, but they remain within us and are not spoken or otherwise outwardly expressed. We talk to God through our minds and share with him our deepest thoughts and sentiments. Although spiritual writers have developed many methods of Christian meditation—the Spiritual Exercises of St. Ignatius of Loyola (1491–1556) being a noteworthy example—they all involve pondering the mysteries of our faith, getting in touch with our feelings about them, finding their relevance for our lives, and making concrete resolutions to do something about them. When Christians meditate, they are talking to God with words, thoughts, and feelings—all within their minds. Meditation, or mental prayer, engages the intellectual and affective side of our human makeup. It is one of the primary ways in which we lift our minds and hearts to God.[10]

Contemplatio, or contemplation, is wordless prayer. It converses with God in silence on the level of the spirit. It feels no need to use words and feelings, but is satisfied simply with resting in the presence of God in quiet. The *Catechism of the Catholic Church* describes it as "a *gaze* of faith, fixed on Jesus," and cites the example of a certain peasant of Ars who, when speaking to St. John Vianney (1786–1859), described his prayer before the Tabernacle in this way: "I look at him, and he looks at me" (no. 2715). Gazing silently upon an icon, or centering prayer, which involves repeating a brief word such as "Jesus" or "Love" over and over to still the heart so it can rest in the silence of God, are good examples of contemplative prayer. Such prayer seeks to communicate with God not on the level of thought, memory, imagination, or feeling but in the peaceful solitude of one's heart. It feels no need to speak to God, but simply gazes upon him in silence and allows God to gaze upon us in return.[11]

Liturgia, or liturgy, is the church at prayer, the people of God—both living and dead—coming together as a believing community to worship God in thanksgiving, praise, and adoration. It is the official, public worship of the church and focuses on the celebration of the sacraments and the Divine Office. The church is most itself when it celebrates the Eucharist, the "sacrament of sacraments" and "the source and summit of the Christian life." This sacrament immerses those present in the saving mystery of Christ's passion, death, and resurrection. When properly celebrated, the church's liturgy engages every dimension of our human makeup: the physical, mental, spiritual, and social. It praises God through words, song, gestures, art, smell, sight, thought, memory, imagination, affection, silence, and rest. And it does so together, in community, for it recognizes that we are all brothers and sisters and members of God's family. It encompasses vocal prayer, meditation, and contemplation—and so very much more. It is the prayer of Christ and his body, the church, offering glory, praise, and adoration to the Father and in the Spirit on every level of his glorified being.[12]

Diverse as they are, the ways of prayer are united by their deep desire to enter into an intimate relationship with the Lord. We pray not only because we love God and wish to befriend him, but also because we believe he loves us and wishes to befriend us in return. Although they may express it differently, the various ways of prayer all seek to enter into close, intimate conversation with God. The person at prayer seeks nothing more (or less) than communion with God. As two friends can communicate with one another in a variety of ways, so the friends of God employ speech, thought, silence, and communal gatherings as a way of sharing with him their innermost thoughts, feelings, troubles, and concerns. Prayer gives a person a way of intimate sharing with God and opens up the way of friendship. In the spiritual life, prayer is like breathing. We must pray at all times; otherwise, we run the risk of spiritual suffocation and our spirits, minds, and hearts become withered and dried.

Conclusion

According to Irenaeus of Lyons (d. 180), "[t]he glory of God is man fully alive."[13] To be fully alive means to have experienced in our lives the fullness of redemption, to have allowed every dimension of our human makeup to be touched by the saving and transforming power of God's grace. For this to happen, we must have ongoing recourse to prayer, "the great means of salvation,"[14] for it is the key that unlocks the door to the abundance of Christ's saving mysteries.

Prayer is not an accessory or an accidental "add-on" to the Christian journey, but part and parcel for its successful completion. It is morally necessary for salvation, meaning that, without it, we can reach our final destination only with great difficulty. According to Alphonsus de Liguori (1696–1787), "[h]e who prays is certainly saved."[15] To this startling and very human assertion, he adds: "There is nothing easier than prayer.

What does it cost us to say, My God, help me! Lord assist me! Have mercy on me! Is there anything more easy than this? And this little will suffice to save, if we will be diligent in doing it"[16] Prayer is easy, however, not because of our own inborn capacity (as if it were just another activity we do like eating or drinking, reading or writing), but on account of the abundance of God's grace made possible by Christ's passion, death, and resurrection. Since it requires faith (itself a gift from God), prayer is not a merely human work, but a concerted action of God and human being. It is not something we do completely on our own; it takes place only when we cooperate with God's grace and enter into intimate conversation with him.

The ways of prayer are as diverse as the various aspects of human existence itself. The physical, mental, spiritual, and social dimensions of prayer are all interrelated and culminate whenever the church gathers for liturgy. By its very nature, Christian prayer leads to the celebration of Eucharist and has its origins in it. The conversation of the two disciples with Jesus on the road to Emmaus brings them eventually to their discovery of him in the breaking of the bread, an experience that sends them running back to the community of disciples they left behind in Jerusalem. Once the two disciples begin conversing with Jesus, everything begins to change. The same can be said for us and anyone else who yearns to follow the way of the Lord Jesus. If we enter into sincere, heartfelt conversation with the Lord, our lives will gradually begin to change—and we will eventually find ourselves running back toward Jerusalem.

The story bolsters our attachment to the Eucharist as the center of Christian life and practice. The disciples at Emmaus recognize Jesus during the breaking of the bread. The eucharistic overtones of this passage invite us to examine our own understanding of what takes place during the eucharistic celebration. During this sacred liturgical action, Christ comes to us in a special way, making himself present to us through the Scriptures, in the breaking of the bread, in the worshiping community, and in the person of the priest and ministers. The popularity of the story is directly related to the Christian community's understanding of the centrality of the eucharistic celebration for the Christian community. During it, we too are given a glimpse of the Risen Christ and confirm our faith in his presence in our midst.

ON THE ROAD TO EMMAUS

■ How do you pray to Jesus?

■ Do you feel most comfortable simply speaking to him?

■ Do you converse with him in your mind and heart?

■ Do you simply rest in his presence?

■ Do you seek him in the presence of others?

■ Do you seek him in liturgy?

■ Do you seek him with your whole heart, mind, soul, and strength?

MY BURNING HEART

Lord, sometimes I just don't know how to talk to you. I find it difficult to share my heart with you, because I am out of touch with my own thoughts and feelings and don't know what to say. Teach me how to pray. Help me to be myself before you. I don't want to put on a mask or pretend I am something I am not. Help me to relate to you as I truly am, without any airs or pretensions. Help me to know my mind and heart, share it with you, and listen in silence for your loving response.

CHAPTER THREE

SEARCHING *the* SCRIPTURES

The way of discipleship involves searching for Jesus in the revealed word of God. For Christians, an intrinsic connection exists between the Scriptures, the word of God as it was disclosed to Moses and the prophets, and Jesus Christ, the Word of God made flesh. This relationship touches the very heart of the Christian faith and is the main reason why Christians retain the Hebrew Scriptures as a part of the canon of their Scriptures. Talk of an Old and a New Testament makes sense only because of the belief that Jesus Christ has inaugurated a fundamental shift in the way God relates to humanity. Christians embrace this fundamental change in outlook. They view themselves as people of the New Covenant. They call themselves "Christians," because they consider Jesus Christ the fullness of God's revelation who sheds light on everything appearing both before and after his appearance in human history. They view the Hebrew Scriptures as a foreshadowing of Christ and interpret them in the light of their faith. For them, Jesus Christ offers an interpretive key for unlocking the meaning of God's word. The story of the two disciples on the road to Emmaus emphasizes this important truth and gave the early Christian communities a deep sense of confidence in Jesus' presence among them.

Finding Jesus in the Word

How is this reflected in Luke's account? After approaching the two disciples on the road, walking with them, asking them about their conversation, and listening to them recount the events surrounding his own death and burial, Jesus confronts them for their lack of wisdom:

> "Oh, how foolish you are, and how slow of heart to believe all that prophets have declared! Was it not necessary that the Messiah should suffer these things and then enter into his glory?" Then beginning with

> Moses and all the prophets, he interpreted to them
> the things about himself in all the scriptures.
>
> ▧ **LUKE 24:25-27**

To understand the impact these verses would have on Luke's readers, it is important to remember that the phrase "Moses and all the prophets" was a way the Jews had of referring to the entirety of their Scriptures. For the people of the New Covenant, however, Jesus reveals the true meaning of these sacred texts, even though, like the two disciples on the road to Emmaus, they often fail to recognize him as he accompanies them on their journey.

What is Luke getting at here? The implications seem clear enough. Jesus remains, at one and the same time, both unrecognized yet palpably present to his disciples. Scripture, moreover, is an important means through which they encounter Jesus and sense his presence in their midst. Later in the story, they even admit that their hearts were burning within them as he was opening up the Scriptures to them (cf. Luke 24:32). For Luke, the experience of the two disciples holds true for the community of disciples on its journey through time and space: Jesus is present to it, yet in a disguised form, hidden yet also revealed; he accompanies them on their journey, yet remains veiled in mystery beneath the words of Scripture. Centuries later, Augustine of Hippo (354–430) would capture this sentiment of the believing community in these striking words: "For now treat the Scripture of God as the face of God. Melt in its presence."[17]

For Christians, the primary purpose of Scripture is to reveal the face of God and mediate a personal encounter with him. That face, they believe, has been given distinct, visible features in the person of Jesus of Nazareth. This insight changes their entire outlook on reality. Scripture, for them, is the revealed word of God, and Jesus is the fullness of that revelation: the two are inseparably linked. Jesus presents himself in the Emmaus story as both the fulfillment of Scripture and its primary interpreter. In explaining the Scriptures to the two disciples, he shows them that the Messiah had to suffer and die in order to enter into his glory. Everything he says suggests that he himself is the long-awaited Messiah and that the recent events of Jerusalem simply had to take place for him to fulfill his heavenly purpose. Jesus interprets the Scripture for his disciples and reveals to them everything in it that refers to him.

The same holds true today. Christians believe that Jesus continues to unlock the mysteries of God's word through the influence of his Spirit, whose ongoing, abiding presence was given to the community of believers at Pentecost (cf. Acts 2). They believe that the Spirit of Christ accompanies them on their journey and continues to reveal to them the hidden face of God. Catholics, moreover, believe that this same Spirit inspires their leaders, the church's magisterium, to safeguard the authentic interpretation of the Scriptures in all things necessary for salvation.

Interpreting God's Word Today

The Emmaus story has great relevance today, for the Bible still remains the single most widely read book in the world. For most people, however, the words of Scripture also number among the most difficult to understand. Although today's methods of exegesis do a fine job in presenting the actual historical context of the revealed word of God, they are rather weak when it comes to drawing out the significance of this information for the spiritual life of the ordinary reader. Understanding the reasons for this inadequacy will help the believer to devise more practical ways of applying the Scriptures to his or her everyday life. The Emmaus story reminds us that Scripture is meant, first and foremost, as a way of mediating an experience of God and should be interpreted in the light of faith seeking understanding.

What does this mean when it comes to searching for the meaning of Scripture? Probably the most notable cause for the lack of spiritual sensitivity in today's biblical exegesis is its exaggerated focus on the literal meaning of the text. This extreme emphasis on the literal sense is an unfortunate by-product of the great success story of the historical-critical method. This scientific approach to the Scriptures was developed during the Age of Enlightenment as part of a well-intentioned but inherently flawed quest for the historical Jesus. Today, it focuses on the written words of the text from a variety of perspectives: textual, source, literary, form, and redaction criticisms—to name but a few. The primary goal of these highly specialized scientific disciplines is to uncover the life situation (*Sitz im Leben*) and literary intention of the authors of the biblical texts. In doing so, they offer the reader a firm hermeneutical basis for reading and understanding the whole of the Scriptures.

By providing a thorough knowledge of the historical situation of the biblical text, the historical-critical method has become the commonly accepted starting point for any serious study of the revealed word of God. But it can only be just that—a starting point. By focusing so much on the scientific analysis of the literal meaning of the text, this method has been granted by some commentators almost exclusive rights over what constitutes a legitimate interpretation of the Scriptures. In doing so, it neglects the other senses of Scripture that focus on the equally (if not more) important spiritual meaning of God's word.

When viewed in the context of the entire history of biblical interpretation, this narrowing of the meaning of Scripture to a scientific analysis of its literal sense is a fairly recent development. Prior to the Enlightenment, Jewish and Christian commentators alike acknowledged the existence of various spiritual senses that complemented the literal meaning of the text and were thought to bring out the fullest meaning of God's revealed word. In Christian thought, for example, patristic and medieval theologians recognized at least four distinct levels of meaning in the sacred texts:

1. the *literal*, which conveyed the historical truth of God's word;

2. the *allegorical*, which dealt with the meaning of God's word in relation to Christ and his church;

3. the *tropological* (or *moral*), which dealt with specific moral truths communicated by God's word; and

4. the *anagogical*, which treated those things having to do with the end times.

These complex terms are actually very easy to understand and have guided Christian interpreters of Scripture since the age of the church fathers. The *literal* sense is the meaning of Scripture "at face value." It represents the most obvious meaning of the text and, for this reason, is usually the easiest to understand. The other three senses of Scripture are known as "the spiritual senses." To see and understand them, we need to ponder the text and ask God for enlightenment. The *allegorical* sense, for example, has to do with the creedal or doctrinal meaning of the text. The *tropological* (or *moral*) sense reveals to us something relevant to human nature and appropriate ethical conduct. The *anagogical* sense tells us something about human destiny and the end times.[18]

These different levels are summed up in the Latin phrase of unknown origin: "*Littera gesta docet, quid credas allegoria/ Moralis quid agas, quo tendas anagogia.*" ("The Letter speaks of deeds; Allegory to faith; the Moral how to act; Anagogy our destiny.")[19] The easiest way to see how these senses operate is to look at the word "Jerusalem." This word appears over nine hundred times in Old and New Testaments. At any one moment, it can be interpreted as the earthly city Jerusalem (the *literal* sense), the church (the *allegorical* sense), the human soul (the *tropological* or *moral* sense), or the heavenly city (the *anagogical* sense).[20] The meaning of the entire passage of Scripture one is reading will change depending on which level the reader understands the term. These various senses of Scripture give witness to the richness of God's word. They invite us to delve beneath the surface of the text and to seek spiritual nourishment from it at every point. Those of us wishing to enter more deeply into the mystery of God's word should be sensitive to these various senses and look for them every time we open the Bible and seek to understand what God might be saying to us. According to traditional practice, a single verse of Scripture could convey one, two, or any combination of these senses. Even today, references to the spiritual meaning of the text are not uncommon in Catholic magisterial documents.

Some Practical Guidelines

It would be foolish to think that Jesus opened the Scriptures to the two disciples on the road to Emmaus solely by employing the textual strategies associated with the historical-critical method. On the contrary, the story itself clearly places the key to unlocking the meaning of Scripture not on the cold calculations of a scientific method, but on the person of Jesus himself. If anything, it encourages a contemplative reading of the text, one that presupposes a living relationship with Christ that interprets the whole of Scripture in the light of his paschal mystery.

This is not the place to get into the various reasons for today's exegetical fixation on the literal meaning of the text. Suffice it to say that changes in the concepts of rationality and the nature of human knowledge have narrowed the field of what many of today's competent exegetes would constitute as a genuine interpretation of the biblical text. This narrowing of the senses of Scripture has opened up a great hunger in the hearts of sincere believers who value the achievements of the historical-critical method and yet cannot help but feel as though something important is missing. What follows are some practical guidelines for anyone interested in unlocking some of the deeper spiritual meanings of the biblical text. They are based on the assumption that a sensitivity to these spiritual senses will complement and even enhance a rigorous analysis of the literal sense. In this respect, the literal and spiritual senses are not competing truths but different aspects of the one revealed truth of God's revelation to humanity. Together, they open up the meaning of Scripture in a way that touches the heart and reveals the face of God to the community of believers.

When you open the Bible, remember that God is its primary author and that his express purpose may not have been immediately evident to his chosen human instruments. In the writing of God's word, these secondary authors used whatever means available to express the mystery of his revelation to his people. These means were often limited in their scope and unable to capture the full import of God's revealed word. In a particular scriptural text, therefore, God's intention may go beyond what the historical-critical method can say about the express intention of the actual human authors themselves.

....

Remember that the entire Bible is the inspired and revealed word of God. Although it contains a variety of forms and literary genres—from poetry to historical narrative to parable (all of which must be duly considered in their proper literary context)—their very arrangement and order is inspired by the Spirit and therefore open to varying forms of comparisons and cross-referencings. In this respect, the meaning of a particular verse of Scripture must be understood not only in the context of the particular literary genre in which it is found, but also in the light of the whole of God's word. When interpreting the Bible, nothing can replace the thorough familiarity with the Scriptures that comes from a balanced regimen of biblical meditation and spiritual reading.

....

Be familiar with what today's biblical criticism has to say about the particular text under consideration. You should always begin with a thorough knowledge of the historical background of the literal sense and use this as the starting point for further reflection. Use these insights as a means of deepening your understanding of the historical situation of the biblical authors. Look for any parallels with your own life situation and try to see what message there is for you on this most fundamental of all levels of meaning.

....

Once you have devoted ample time to the literal sense, put your Bible aside for the moment and ask God to help you to discern some of the deeper spiritual meanings of the text. Spend some time in silence. Get in touch with your deepest cares and concerns. Ask God to help you understand what the passage might have to say to you at this particular moment in your life. After a few moments of quiet centering prayer, reopen your Bible and read the text again, very slowly, this time concentrating on every word. Allow your mind to associate freely with every person, circumstance, and image that passes through your mind as you read and then reread the text. Ask God to give you a deeper understanding of yourself and your relationship to him. Concentrate on whatever free associations may come, and try to understand why they came to mind in the context of this particular text from Scripture. You are now beginning to delve beneath the literal sense and allowing the Scripture to touch your personal life.

....

If you have any hesitation about the validity of the allegorical interpretation of the Scriptures, realize that there are

a number of places even within the New Testament where such an approach is used and even put on the lips of Jesus to underscore its legitimacy (e.g., Mark 4:13–20; Matthew 13:36–43). While care must be taken to avoid undue exaggeration even with this method of interpretation, do not be afraid to discern parallel patterns either within the various texts of the Scriptures themselves (e.g., from one book to another) or between the Scriptures and the theological tradition of the church (the Scriptures, after all, would not even exist were it not for its intimate relation with the living tradition of the church). In Greek, the word "allegory" means "to say something other." Do not be surprised to find a particular verse of Scripture conveying "something other" than its most obvious meaning. The more the interpretation can be confirmed by other references from either within the Scriptures themselves or the tradition of the church, the more weight should be given to it.

....

Use the text as the basis for a theological reflection on the person of Christ and of his love for the People of God, the church. In addition to the traditional images that have been used to explain the relationship between Christ and his church (e.g., head and body; groom and bride), try to be open to any new themes that express in a more powerful way for today's world the nature of Christ's redemptive mission (e.g., Jesus as healer, liberator, brother). Do not force the associations. Let them simply arise through your quiet pondering on the meaning of God's word. If nothing comes after a minute or two, leave this level of reflection for the next with the hope of coming back to it later. Remember that not every verse has to have a Christological or ecclesiological meaning associated with it. At the same time, you must try to be sensitive to those that really do.

....

The next level of spiritual meaning is the moral or ethical sense. Ask yourself what the text has to say to you about the way to live your life. Does it give any explicit moral exhortations? Does it convey any implicit connotations on how the Christian life should be lived? Are these suggestions relevant to living the Christian life in the modern world? Read the text again and ask God to show you the areas in your life that you need to work on. Close your eyes and ponder the words of the text. Let them speak to your life and realize that the word of God carries a personal message for each individual. "Ask, and it will be given you; search, and you will find; knock, and the door will be opened for you" (Matthew 7:7).

....

Now consider the text in relation to what it might have to say about the last things such as death, judgment, resurrection, heaven, and hell. Use this moment as a point of reflection on your own death, and ask God to give you the strength and the courage to be true to him until the very end. Remember all those who have touched your life and who have already gone before you marked by the sign of faith. Allow these people to pass through your mind. Picture them reading the text with you, and ask God to help you understand something more about the mystery of death and how it touches the redemptive mystery of Christ's own death and burial. Realize that, by virtue of being the inspired word of God, every verse of Scripture has some kind of eschatological orientation. If no explicit insight comes to mind, know that merely reflecting on the passage in light of the ultimate realities of the faith will put you in deeper touch with the challenge of Christian discipleship.

Be open to more recent forms of biblical exegesis that utilize a fundamentally allegorical (i.e., "saying something other") approach to the text. The insights of Jungian dream interpretation or the Enneagram, for example, can be used with great success as a means of breaking through the literal core of the biblical text in order to share in a deeper understanding of the unconscious forces involved in the very writing of the inspired word of God itself. "The wind blows where it chooses..." (John 3:8). Do not be surprised when such recently developed methods of interpretation open up new vistas and ways of looking at God's word. At the same time, use such methods in a complementary fashion to the well-tried means of traditional scriptural exegesis. God's word is so rich that the Spirit can use virtually any method of interpretation to communicate some insight into the meaning that God wishes to convey.

....

Finally, always return to the literal sense of the text. Gather whatever insights you have gained from the above steps, and weigh them in light of the initial findings of the historical-critical method. Correlate whatever contradictions may appear, and try to reconcile them either in direct relation to one another or by placing them on different levels of the one truth of God's revealed word. In doing so, you are bringing the interpretative act full circle and may be surprised to find that many fit well together and will actually help you to form a meaningful composite of what the word of God has to say to you at this particular moment in your life.

These suggestions are intended to help the believer gain a more profound insight into the meaning of God's word and to discover the vast spiritual treasures that lie just beneath its surface. Their goal is to give the reader a deeper appreciation of the spiritual senses of Scripture and to show how these deeper levels of meaning can nourish the human spirit and enliven the soul in times of difficulty. In doing so, they should move the reader to an even deeper appreciation of the literal meaning of the text and encourage him or her to use the insights of the historical-critical method to even better avail. They also seek to help the reader imagine that Jesus himself is involved in the interpretive process and that he himself is accompanying the reader on his or her own journey to Emmaus and, as in the case of the two disciples, revealing insights that burn their hearts within and touch the core of their being.

Conclusion

In the story of the two disciples on the road to Emmaus, Jesus interprets the whole of Scripture in the light of his paschal mystery. He embodies in himself the interpretive key that unlocks the meaning of Holy Writ. The two disciples come to a deeper understanding of the Scriptures because they listen to Jesus as he engages them in conversation and discloses to them the meaning of the words in a way that sets their hearts on fire.

One of the greatest threats to interpreting the Scriptures in a mature way is the tendency some readers have for claiming exclusive rights for a single method in expounding the meaning of God's word. This threat is as much a problem for the more traditional spiritual approach (which has been known, at times, to separate itself from the literal sense) as for the historical-critical method (which has often accused this alternative approach of unjustly reading into the text). Rather than concentrating on the mistakes of the past, today's Bible interpreter should focus more on the ways in which these different methods actually complement each other and use them together in a prudent and prayerful manner.

Most Christians open the Bible not so much for its intellectual content (formidable though it may be) but to come to know God in a more intimate way and hopefully to receive a deeper insight into the direction his or her life should take.

By using the various spiritual senses of Scripture as a way of delving beneath the insights of the literal meaning of the text, this person can have a deeper experience of the inspired word and thus be better prepared to recognize the quiet movement of God in his or her life.

In the final analysis, the mystery of God's word cannot be exhausted by a single method of interpretation. By using more than one approach to the Scriptures, there is always more of a chance that a person will arrive at a deeper understanding of the text. This can only be of help to those who want to integrate their reading of Scripture with the problems of their daily lives. Christians in the modern world surely need all the help they can get. The story of the two disciples on the road to Emmaus offers some key insights into how Jesus reveals himself to his disciples and sets their hearts ablaze.

ON THE ROAD TO EMMAUS

- What do you expect to find when you open up the Scriptures?
- How do you interpret it?
- Do you invite Jesus into your reading?
- Do you pray over what you read?
- Do you stay on the surface of the text?
- Do you seek the text's deeper, spiritual meaning?
- Do you seek its relevance for your life?

MY BURNING HEART

Lord, sometimes I feel as though I take the Scriptures for granted. I don't spend enough time with them and sometimes even doubt if you have anything to say to me through them. I say they are sacred words, but I treat them like any other piece of literature. Help me to reverence your word. Help me to ponder it and spend time with it. Help me to break it open, meditate upon it, and allow your Spirit to help me see its deeper meaning. Help me to find its relevance for my life. Help me to allow your word to burn within my heart.

CHAPTER FOUR

OUR BEFRIENDING LORD

I n the Emmaus story, Jesus accompanies the two disciples and befriends them on their journey. Within a very short time, he forges a bond with them that gradually passes from his being a mere stranger, to a fellow traveler, to a welcome guest at table. By accompanying them along the way, he enters into a personal relationship with them and affords them the opportunity to get to know him. He befriends them at a time in their lives when they are confused by recent events and uncertain about their future. He meets them where they are and kindles hope in their hearts in the midst of their despondency. What is more, he is the one who takes the initiative by drawing near to them, walking with them, and engaging them in conversation. During this time, he not only walks and talks with them, but also draws close to them, so much so that at the journey's end, *they* take the initiative and invite him to stay with them. Something has happened to these two disciples as Jesus befriends them on the way. After meeting him, their lives are never the same. Friendship with him makes all the difference in the world.

The Bond of Friendship

Friendship can best be characterized as a close bond between two individuals by virtue of some common interest.[21] This interest provides the focal point for their common gaze and allows each individual to stand beside the other on an equal footing. A friendship can form around almost anything. In the case of the two disciples on the road to Emmaus, the common basis for their friendship is their love for the Lord. Immersed in a common interest, friends are able to overlook the typical social stereotyping often made on the basis of religion, sex, race, or economic class. They are able to do so because of one important discovery. "He (or she) actually enjoys doing the same thing I do!" Little else matters.

In some ways, friendship (*philia* in Greek) is the most difficult to grasp of the natural human loves. Unlike romantic love (*eros*), which focuses on the mutual experience of "being in love" (for example, two lovers staring into each other's eyes), or simple affection (*storge*), which stems from natural instincts at work in well-established relationships (for example, a mother's affection for her child), friendship is based solely on the selfless absorption in a subject of common interest. That is not to say that lovers cannot be the best of friends or that a father cannot befriend his son. The point is that such friendships will exist only when these individuals discover a common interest. Thus, two lovers will appreciate each other as friends when they realize that they share a love for, say, classical music or horseback riding; the father and his son, in turn, will draw close because of their fever for fishing or baseball, stamp collecting, or what have you. The natural human loves (affection, romantic love, and friendship) have been known to complement each other in these and other diverse ways.[22]

Friendship's great strength is its general openness toward those wishing to share in the subject of common interest. This openness forms the basis for other friendships. We see this openness reflected in the two disciples as they welcome a stranger in their midst, allow him to accompany them on their journey, and bring him into their conversation. As the circle of friends grows, each individual has a particular insight into his or her subject and is appreciated for offering it. Everyone has a unique contribution to make. Equally admirable is the way the bond developed from a common interest expands into other areas and, as the friendship strengthens, manifests itself in a genuine and active concern for the well-being of a friend. A true friend, says Proverbs 18:24, is more loyal than a brother.

As for its weaknesses, if they are not careful, those involved in a friendship can be indifferent toward those who do not share their common interests. Friends can also become inflated with pride and consider themselves superior to those outside their comfortable circle. When allowed to persist, such weaknesses will turn a group of friends into an introverted clique of self-complacent individuals. Such friendships are really not friendships at all and can hardly be elevated by God to a higher plane.

Probing More Deeply

It may be helpful at this point to leave the Emmaus story momentarily and highlight some of the key insights about friendship in the West's philosophical and theological tradition. The Greek philosopher Aristotle (384–322 BC) and the medieval Cistercian abbot Aelred of Rievaulx (1109–1167) immediately come to mind.

In his *Nicomachean Ethics*, Aristotle describes three different kinds of friendship, all of which stem from three possible motivations: utility, pleasure, and character.[23] Propelled by some vested interest that dictates the parameters of the relationship, we enter into *friendships of utility* in order to get something for ourselves. We become friends with another person only because he or she is of some use to us. Utility is the common motivation; when the motivation ceases, so does the friendship. *Friendships of pleasure*, by way of contrast, develop because we enjoy being in a certain person's company. We like being with a particular individual because he or she makes us laugh, engages us in thoughtful conversation, is good dinner company, etc. We relish being with him or her—and vice versa. Pleasure is the common motivation: nothing more; nothing less. In such friendships, we appreciate not the friend but the pleasure he or she bestows on us. Despite their familiar presence in our lives, friendships of utility and pleasure fall far short of perfection. When someone no longer benefits us or ceases to evoke in us any pleasure, it is relatively easy for us to stop caring for him or her. These kinds of friendships can easily form—and just as easily dissolve. They lack the staying power of firm, solid friendships. Completely on the other side of the spectrum are *friendships of character*. In these relationships, we wish the well-being of our friend for his or her own sake. Our love for the Good is what draws us together and keeps us united through thick and through thin. Becoming good by living the virtuous life is the common motivation. Once forged, such friendships do not dwindle or fade. They last a lifetime.

Aristotle goes on to provide three characteristics of true friendships:

1. benevolence, where we not only wish our friends well, but also actually seek their well-being;

2. reciprocity, which insists on a mutual rapport between friends and warns of the dangers of one-sided relationships; and

3. mutual indwelling, which enables each friend to see himself or herself reflected in the other as another self.[24]

Let us look at each of these in turn.

True friendship requires a person to actively seek the well-being of another. This means more than simply wishing the other person well or helping him or her in time of need. It means putting oneself in the other person's shoes and making a conscious effort to do whatever it takes to help that person along. Benevolence requires active listening, a generous heart, and a creative imagination. It means making a friend's good one's own and doing all one can to help that friend achieve it. Without benevolence, potential friendships never get off the ground; they founder for lack of concern and err too much on the side of caution.

True friendship is mutual; giving and receiving are part and parcel of the relationship. This means that each friend actively pursues the well-being of the other. If this does not occur, an unhealthy situation can arise where one person takes unfair advantage of the other's good intentions. The results can be devastating, especially when the relationship ends abruptly. A true friend offers himself or herself to another and fully expects that friend to do the same. That is not to say that the concrete expressions of friendship will be commensurate. Nor does it mean that friends should waste their time keeping a record of what they do (and not do) for each other. A friend does what he or she can to ensure the other's welfare. Just what that should be is known only to that individual—and to God.

True friends carry each other with them wherever they go. Time and space may separate them physically but not spiritually. They dwell in each other's hearts. They have gotten to know each other so well that each becomes a vivid reflection of the other. This second self offers support and receives it; it knows when to push and when to be patient; it offers unconditional love for the other and receives it in return. "Faithful friends are a sturdy shelter" (Sirach 6:14). We offer our friends the shelter of our hearts. The warmth we share as a result enables us not merely to survive, but to thrive in the most difficult of circumstances.

Because of their coherency and near universal appeal, these insights have sometimes been used by theologians to shed light on the meaning of Christian friendship. For example, Thomas Aquinas (1224/25–1274), the great thirteenth-century Dominican theologian, likens charity to "a certain friendship with God" that displays each of these important characteristics.[25] A person who is a friend of God shares an intimate relationship with him and lives a life of charity. To be a friend of God is to share in the inner life of God, to participate in the benevolent, reciprocal, and mutually indwelling love of the Trinity itself.

In his twelfth-century classic, *Spiritual Friendship*, Aelred of Rievaulx outlines four qualities of a genuine, God-centered friendship: love, affection, security, and happiness.[26] Love, for Aelred, means being there for our friends when they need us and showing our concern for their welfare. Affection means revealing our inward feelings in outward signs and gestures. Security fosters an atmosphere of trust that enables us to reveal our innermost thoughts without fear and suspicion. Happiness enables us to share everything with our friends: the good, the bad, and the ugly. These four qualities are present wherever God is the common interest that forges genuine bonds of human friendship. They are present in all true spiritual friendships, especially in those that bear the name "Christian."

These characteristics may seem too idealistic, too out-of-touch, or too unrealistic in the humdrum of modern existence. Perhaps they are. But perhaps that is part of the problem. Perhaps we have lost touch with the great art of making friends. Perhaps we are too busy. A spiritual friendship does not simply happen. It is hard work. It requires a long process of discernment. Later in his treatise, Aelred outlines four stages by which one enters into friendship with another: selection, probation, admission, and union.[27] As far as the first is concerned, he wonders why it is we hesitate when it comes to selecting our friends when we are so good at selecting just about every other necessity of life. Since not everyone is worthy of our trust, we should subject a person to intense scrutiny before we decide to go any further. The second stage, that of probation, involves a process of building up a sense of mutual trust so that four essential qualities can be tested:

a) loyalty, whereby a person learns to trust his or her friend securely;

b) right intention, whereby a person's friend comes to expect nothing from the friendship but God and its natural good;

c) discretion, whereby a person learns when to encourage and when to correct a friend; and

d) patience, whereby a friend learns to not bear hard feelings when confronted and to bear every adversity for the sake of the other.

In the third stage, that of admission, we finally recognize that we have become friends, and we refer to each other as such. It is here where we have to speak of different levels of friendship. Aelred himself recognizes a movement from being an acquaintance, to a companion, to a friend, to the most cherished of friends. Perhaps each of us should ask ourselves, *What are the different levels of friendships in my life? Who are my acquaintances? Who are my companions? My friends? My most cherished friends?* The fourth stage, that of union, is perfect harmony in all things. Here, the friend becomes another self: "a single soul in two bodies." What happens to one's friend happens to oneself—and vice versa. The bond cannot be broken.

The Dimensions of Spiritual Friendship

If we return to the Emmaus story, we see that it is very much about Jesus befriending the two disciples on the road and being befriended by them in return. Christianity, in fact, proposes a threefold order of friendship. First, there is the community of friends in the Godhead itself: Father, Son, and Spirit bonded together by their love of what is One, Good, True, and Beautiful; all seek each other's well-being, reciprocate their love for one another, and mutually indwell each other in an intimate embrace of love. Then, there is the individual's friendship with God. The same three characteristics resonate in my relationship with the ground of my being. God seeks my well-being, and I seek God's; we nurture a close, mutual rapport with one another; God dwells in me, and I dwell in God. Finally, there is friendship among Christians themselves. United by their common interest in and friendship with God, Christians forge genuine bonds of friendship that enable them constantly to seek each other's interest in a respectful, reciprocal manner, in the hope of becoming a reflection of the other's love for God. Each of these orders, moreover, somehow interrelates. As the Emmaus story demonstrates, the befriending God fosters befriending Christians, who live in turn for the purpose of fostering an ever-widening circle of God's friends. Christian friendship is one of the most precious treasures a person can be given. "Faithful friends are a sturdy shelter" (Sirach 6:14). "A true friend sticks closer than one's nearest kin" (Proverbs 18:24). "No one has greater love than this, to lay down one's life for one's friends" (John 15:13).

What does all this say about our befriending God? It tells us that he is a quiet, unpretentious partner in all genuine human friendships. He makes possible even the smallest gathering of friends by merely keeping us in existence, even where a mere two or three are gathered. For the most part, he is content with playing a supporting role in the development of such wholesome human friendships. Among his many interests, one in particular must be watching people become good friends. Given the great numbers of friends present in the world today (and throughout history), it is probably fair to conclude that it ranks as one of his favorite spectator pastimes.

As friendships deepen, it is not uncommon for people to become more and more aware of the presence of this silent third party. This unobtrusive partner will never bully his way onto center stage. He must be invited. Only then will he come out of his position as a silent spectator and take a more prominent role in a relationship of friends. For some friends, this may amount to nothing more than the tacit recognition that their common interest or activity holds something of transcendent value. Others will sense a personal presence in the silence that forms the backdrop of their common activity. Still others will try to name it and, in doing so, come to a deeper recognition of the elusive nature of this silent player. By befriending that silence, friends embrace God himself as the source of their common interest and ground of their friendship. At such a moment, the friendship itself is consciously focused on God and merits to have the modifier "spiritual" placed before it.

While no two spiritual friendships are exactly alike, each contains a threefold orientation toward God, other, and self. Love of the Father is the common concern upon which the first is based. As Jesus tells his disciples, "I have called you friends, because I have made known to you everything that I have heard from my Father" (John 15:15). For Christians, this personal love for God the Father is mediated through the person of Jesus who, in turn, provides the common faith experience that joins two believers in a relationship of spiritual friendship. "If you knew me, you would know my Father also" (John 8:19). Jesus is also the basis upon which each individual integrates the various aspects of the self and learns to befriend and understand them. "Whoever follows me will never walk in darkness..." (John 8:12).

The binding force on each and every one of these levels is the Holy Spirit, who is the bond uniting the Son to the Father, Jesus to his disciples, and the believer to an integrated understanding of the self. The Spirit expresses itself on each of these levels through the practice of divine self-giving, i.e., the virtue of Christian charity (*agape*). Focused on the Father, befriended by Christ, and bonded by the Spirit, spiritual friendship highlights the Trinitarian dimensions of human existence. It seeks to make the love of Father, Son, and Spirit a concrete reality in the lives of two disciples and, because such love is naturally self-diffusive, in a host of many others.

Conclusion

The story of the two disciples on the road to Emmaus teaches us that spiritual friendship is a shared experience of "being in the Lord." As this experience deepens, it moves of its own accord toward some form of outward, apostolic expression. Without the support of a spiritual friend, this activity can turn quite easily into a stale, mechanical performance of duty. With another person to talk to about both the joys and pains of the apostolate, the work retains its interesting features and becomes far easier to carry out on an ongoing basis. "My yoke is easy, and my burden is light" (Matthew 11:30).

No one is ever fully aware of how Christ manifests himself in human lives. His quiet transformation of natural human friendships is but one of countless ways in which his Spirit visits the human heart. By cooperating with his grace, spiritual friends help to make his love a visible reality in their lives and in the lives of those around them. Like the two disciples at Emmaus, they find themselves running back to Jerusalem to spread the Good News and to animate the life of the local community in any number of ways. As such, they represent some of the untapped potential that the church has at its ready disposal. Let them be recognized and encouraged to grow in the Lord and dispense his bounteous gifts. They will ask for very little in return.

As the Emmaus story teaches us, the desire of spiritual friends to spread the Good News derives from their deep relationship of faith that they share with their Lord, who shelters them and moves them to extend their great joy to others. Spiritual friends are not rare but common occurrences in the life of the church. Most are ordinary, practical people, from all walks of life, who face their worries head-on, one at a time, with a deeply shared love for God. With their lives and their relationship focused on Christ, they look for honest solutions to their problems and seek to lighten the burden of those around them. In a genuine spiritual friendship, little else is of any real concern.

ON THE ROAD TO EMMAUS

- Do you feel befriended by God?
- Do you believe that God actively pursues your well-being?
- Do you reciprocate his love in your thoughts, words, and actions?
- Have you experienced God dwelling in your heart?
- Is your friendship with God reflected in your friendship with others?
- Do you have any close, intimate friends?
- Do they lead you closer to or further away from him?

MY BURNING HEART

Lord, I'm not really sure I understand what friendship is all about. I say I have close friends, but I wonder how many of them really know me. Perhaps it's because I sometimes feel as though I hardly know myself. Lord, I believe that you know me better than I know myself. Help me to place my heart in yours. Come into my life. Dwell within my heart. Show me what it means to be a friend. Help me to befriend others as you have befriended me.

CHAPTER FIVE

In the BREAKING *of the* BREAD

A ccording to the fathers of the Second Vatican Council, the Eucharist is "the source and summit of the Christian life."[28] This sacrament both constitutes the church and is constituted by it. It embraces the whole of Christ's paschal mystery and thus connects Christian life and worship in a way that touches the very heart of discipleship. The Eucharist places those celebrating it in direct contact with Jesus' passion, death, and resurrection.

When the two disciples break bread with Jesus at Emmaus, their eyes are opened, and they recognize him as their Risen Lord. They also come to see the close, intimate relationship between the simple act of breaking bread together and the love Jesus bears them. That love culminates in his death on Golgotha and is made present whenever two or three gather in his name to celebrate the sacrament in memory of him. The Eucharist, for this reason, has often been called the "sacrament of love." It embodies everything that Jesus stands for and wishes for his followers. For them, there can be no separation between liturgy and authentic Christian living. Spirituality and morality, worship and ethics, go hand in hand. To recognize Jesus in the breaking of the bread means that his disciples sense the presence of the Risen Lord in the face of the stranger and in the faces of everyone they encounter on the way.

In the Breaking of the Bread

The Emmaus story is partly about finding Christ in the face of the stranger and partly about finding the stranger in the face of Christ. The two processes go hand in hand. As they near the village, Jesus, still unrecognized by them, is about to take his leave of his companions and continue his journey (v. 28). He does not wish to overstay his welcome or force himself on anyone. If he is not invited to stay, he will simply go on his way. He will remain with them only if they ask him. His companions on the road choose to do so.

It is growing dark, and the two disciples press him to stay with them (v. 29). Perhaps they hope he will continue to teach them and make the words of Scripture come alive for them. Perhaps they feel sorry for him, a stranger traveling all alone on a dark country road. Perhaps they wish to offer him hospitality, a hot meal and a warm bed, before he continues his journey the next day. Jesus agrees and goes in to eat and presumably to take lodging with them. While they are at supper, he takes the bread, pronounces the blessing, breaks it, and begins to distribute it to them (v. 30). At that moment, something happens. Time seems to stand still. A dark veil is lifted from their eyes, and the disciples suddenly recognize the man before them as Jesus, their Master (v. 31).

Unfortunately, they have little, if any, time to react. Before they can think or say or do anything, their companion vanishes from their sight and is nowhere to be found (v. 31). Jesus has come to them, revealed himself, and then quickly taken his leave of them. He has been present to his disciples in a way they had never before experienced. He has disappeared, but they still feel as though he is very close to them. The broken bread on the table before them reminds them of what he had said to his disciples just a few nights before: "This is my body, which is given for you. Do this in remembrance of me" (Luke 22:19). They also remember how their hearts burned within them when he was explaining the Scriptures to them along the road (v. 32). How could they not have recognized him then? What was it that kept them from seeing him in their strange traveling companion? They are suddenly filled with a sense of urgency and purpose (v. 33). Everything in their lives has come together, and they remember that it all took place during the breaking of the bread. And it has ever since.

For centuries, Christians the world over have found their own experience reflected in the experience of these two disciples. Their walk of faith has led them to believe that they too can receive an authentic (if fleeting) glimpse of the Risen Lord whenever they gather for Eucharist. They relive the journey to discipleship whenever they gather in faith for the breaking of the bread. They share that bread with friend and stranger alike, forging relationships rooted in the New Covenant, a pact written in the life, words, and blood of Jesus himself.

The Sacrament of the New Covenant

Jesus' words of blessing as he broke bread with his disciples the evening before his death make little sense unless they are understood as a symbolic representation of a New Covenant existing between God and humanity. The bread and wine he shares with his disciples signify the sacrifice of his body and blood to be given up and poured out for the sake of many. By placing his passion and death in the context of his last Passover meal, Jesus provides his followers with a concrete way of remembrance that exists in continuity with the tradition of their ancestors and that also raises their awareness of a new, definitive action of God in their lives. In this respect, it partakes in those very events that shape his own destiny in the plan of his Father.

Jesus' last meal is linked not only with the events following it, but also with those preceding it. In all three of the synoptic Gospels, his public ministry both begins and ends with a symbolic action: the former, that of his baptism by John in the Jordan (Matthew 3:13–17; Mark 1:9–11; Luke 3:21–22); the latter, that of the first Eucharist (Matthew 26:26–29; Mark 14:22–25; Luke 22:19–20). Even in the Gospel of John, which includes neither Jesus' baptism nor the actual words of institution, the account of his public ministry contains many allusions to the eucharistic banquet, i.e., changing the water into wine at Cana (2:1–12), the miracle of the loaves (6:1–15), his discourse at Capernaum (6:22–66, especially 32–58), the discourse on the vine and the branches (15:1–17), and the meal of bread and fish (21:9–14). The point being made here is that, while Jesus' words of institution (considered authentic even according to the standards of biblical criticism) link the Last Supper with the events of his passion and death, the evangelists (writing under the inspiration of the Holy Spirit) associate it also with the events of his public ministry. The synoptic authors achieve the latter by using the symbolic actions of the Lord's baptism and Last Supper as a means of defining the limits of his public ministry; the author of the Gospel of John does so by filling the account of Jesus' ministry of teaching and healing with numerous eucharistic undertones. In this respect, the Eucharist is connected as much to the life as it is to the death of the Lord Jesus. And, in both cases, they point to what obviously stands out as the culminating event of his life and death, i.e., his resurrection on Easter Sunday morning.

In his use of symbolism as a means of communicating the truth of his redemptive mission, Jesus stands in marked continuity with the long tradition of Hebrew prophetic utterance. Hosea's marriage to the faithless Gomer (Hosea 1:2–9), Jeremiah's symbols of the loincloth (Jeremiah 13:1–11) and the shattered wine jugs (Jeremiah 48:12–13), Ezekiel's making of bread from a single pot of wheat, barley, beans, lentils, millet, and spelt (Ezekiel 4:9), and his mime of the emigrant (Ezekiel 12:1–20) are all examples of the prophetic use of concrete material signs and actions to convey the message of Yahweh to his people. What is so often forgotten when interpreting these actions is that, as authentic utterances of the word of God, they actually bring into effect what they symbolize: God's word does not return in vain (Isaiah 55:11). In this respect, Jesus' breaking of the bread and drinking from the cup in the company of his disciples brings the event of Calvary into their midst. That is to say that, before his actual death, Jesus makes present the redemptive effects of that first Good Friday in the bread and wine he eats and drinks with his disciples. These effects culminate in his Easter rising and, as stated earlier, are already anticipated in his ministry of teaching and healing.[29]

The Emmaus account of the two disciples who experience Jesus in the breaking of the bread affirms Jesus' ongoing presence in the sacrament of the New Covenant. It does so by juxtaposing Jesus' symbolic action of breaking bread with his disciples on the night before his death with one of his early post-resurrection appearances. This juxtaposition brings together the three key aspects of Catholic belief regarding the sacrament: banquet, presence, and sacrifice. Rooted in the long tradition of Hebrew prophetic utterance, the institution of the Eucharist takes place in the context of a sacred meal, in the midst of his disciples, and in a symbolic action that embodies his redemptive suffering and death.

A Threefold Mystery

Asked by Jesus to remember him in this sacred action, his disciples and the communities established by them soon came to recognize that the thanksgiving they rendered to God in their breaking of the bread was a foretaste of the heavenly banquet, a continuing presence of the Risen Lord in their midst, and a sacrifice of Christ's suffering and death. Disagreement over the precise nature of each of these elements and the way in which they interact with one another has been the cause of much unrest and turmoil in the history of the church.

....

The Eucharist as Banquet. At Emmaus, Jesus breaks bread with the two disciples and manifests his true identity to them. Even to the external observer, the relationship that the Eucharist has to the fellowship of a sacred meal is obvious and nearly always presumed. Like the Passover—its Jewish counterpart—the celebration of the Eucharist commemorates the great saving acts of God on behalf of his people. Its purpose is to bond Christians together first through a telling of the great Christian narrative as it has been handed down through the gospels and interpreted by Paul and other apostolic witnesses of the faith, and then through the ritualistic sharing in the bread and cup that Christ himself likened to the eating of his own body and blood. In this respect, the Eucharist serves as a focus of identity for the Christian people.

By remembering the stories and performing the actions that Jesus asked to be done in his memory, they find themselves drawing closer to one another and thus able to build community in what, at times, appears to be the most unlikely of circumstances. As food for wayfaring pilgrims, the Eucharist provides spiritual strength and nourishment for the believing community's earthly pilgrimage in faith. As a foretaste of the heavenly banquet, it preserves the hope that the reign of God manifested in Christ will one day be fully realized in the lives of his followers. It should not be surprising that the Eucharist, when considered as a meal or banquet, receives almost universal acclaim: Christians of all denominations affirm the importance of the great spiritual strength they receive from their gathering in fellowship around the table of the Lord. It was much the same for the disciples at Emmaus.[30]

The Eucharist as Presence. When they reach their destination, the eyes of the two disciples are opened and they recognize Jesus when he says the blessing and breaks bread with them. The Emmaus story affirms that the Risen Christ is present to his followers in numerous ways: in their walk along the road (v. 15), in their discussion of recent events (vv. 16–24), in the explanation of the Scriptures (vv. 25–27), and, most especially, "in the breaking of the bread" (vv. 30–31). The latter involves not only the presence of Jesus, but also an awareness of this presence on the part of his disciples. This recognition comes in the eucharistic action (i.e., "the *breaking of the bread*") and signifies Christ's dynamic personal presence to the community of believers in their celebration of the great commemorative action of his redemptive love: in their remembering, believers recognize the very person of Christ in the midst of the sacramental action for which they are giving thanks.

Christ is present in similar ways even in eucharistic celebrations today: in the coming and going forth; in the explanation of the Scriptures; in the accompanying homiletic reflection; most especially, in the breaking of the bread. Within Catholic circles, a special reverence is given to the presence of Christ in the person of the priest, who consecrates the eucharistic species. Since Vatican II, emphasis has also been placed on the presence of Christ in the worshiping community. While these various presences of Christ in the liturgy do not exist in tension with each other in and of themselves, it is understandable that, for various reasons, persons or communities of differing spiritualities may wish to emphasize one mode of Christ's presence over another (e.g., his presence in the word over his presence in the community). Be that as it may, one of the identifying characteristics of the Roman Catholic Church is an august theological realism that insists with firm religious conviction that, in the eucharistic celebration, the bread and wine are actually changed into the Body and Blood of the Risen Lord.[31]

The Eucharist as Sacrifice. After recognizing him in the breaking of the bread, the two disciples find new meaning in Jesus' suffering and death and rush back to Jerusalem to share the news with the other disciples. When discussing the way in which the eucharistic celebration participates in the sacrifice on Golgotha, the tendency, in Catholic circles, has been to emphasize the eternal aspect of Christ's redemptive act and its ability to enter the realm of history in whatever manner and whatever moment in time. The great strength of this approach is that it joins the action of the Mass to Christ's sacrifice on the cross without turning the former into a historical reenactment of the latter. Catholics have always affirmed the unique, unrepeatable nature of the event of Golgotha; it is precisely because Christ's death extends beyond the bounds of time that it may now be invoked at any point along the continuum of history. Rather than a reenactment of Golgotha, the celebration of the Eucharist is a sacramental realization of what, by all counts, is the veritable culmination of the whole of salvation history. Indeed, what needs to be brought out more in the discussion of the sacrificial aspects of the Eucharist is the way Christ's redemptive offering on Golgotha is made present not only in its reality as an event, but also in the two conditions relating to it by way of cause and effect, i.e., the incarnation and the resurrection. That is to say that the redemptive truth of Christ's bloody death presupposes both the reality of his becoming a man and its causal relationship to his being raised on Easter morning by the power of the Father.

In this respect, the contours of Christ's redemption of humanity encompass his entire life—from the manger to the empty tomb—and are present in the church's celebration of the Eucharist. In this dramatic action, Christ's becoming man, his dying on the cross, and his rising from the dead engage all who partake of the bread that is his Body and the wine that is his Blood. By receiving the Body and Blood of the Risen Lord in the Eucharist, the faithful receive the effects of Christ's redemptive action and are able to carry on his ministry of healing and teaching. From very early on, the community of disciples sensed this intimate connection between Christ's death, his resurrection, and their breaking of bread together. In returning to Jerusalem from Emmaus, the two disciples return to Golgotha, to the empty tomb, and to the community of disciples. From then on, the breaking of the bread would be an integral part of their lives. Everything would flow from it and return to it.[32]

Conclusion

Recognizing Jesus in the breaking of the bread was a turning point in the lives of the two disciples at Emmaus. From the moment they saw him and understood his true identity, nothing again would ever be the same for them. Their encounter with him at table turned their lives around and sent them rushing back toward Jerusalem with their hearts ablaze with the Good News of the Risen Lord. For them, the journey of discipleship would take them back to the place of Jesus' death and burial, to the community of disciples, and to an uncertain future.

No one knows exactly what happened to Cleopas and his companion after their experience of Jesus in the breaking of the bread. After the Emmaus story, they disappear from the pages of history as quickly as Jesus vanished from their sight when he broke bread with them and opened their eyes to see him as he truly was. It is possible, however (even probable), that they became immersed in the life of the community of disciples at Jerusalem. As the Acts of the Apostles affirms, that small, emerging body of the faithful devoted itself "to the apostles' teaching and fellowship, to the breaking of bread and the prayers" (Acts 2:42). Could it be that the experience of the disciples at Emmaus had some part to play in making the breaking of bread a central feature of early Christian practice? Luke seems to think so.

In his gospel, this evangelist draws a clear parallel between Jesus' Last Supper with his disciples and his supper with the two disciples at Emmaus. In the first, Jesus ties the simple action of breaking bread together with his suffering, death, and entrance into the kingdom (Luke 22:16). In the second, he opens the Scripture to his disciples about the meaning of his suffering and death and reveals to them at table that he has indeed entered into his glory (Luke 24:27, 31). In this way, the breaking of bread at the Last Supper and Emmaus serve as "literary bookends" for the telling (and retelling) of Jesus' paschal mystery, thus making the celebration of the Eucharist a central part of early Christian belief and practice.

As mentioned at the outset of this chapter, the Eucharist both constitutes the church and is constituted by it. It lies at the very heart of the Christian kerygma for it is "the source and summit of Christian life." In the ebb and flow of history, it is a constant reminder that Jesus is "Emmanuel," "God with us" (Matthew 1:23). In the life of the church, it is the "sacrament of love" that celebrates Christ's sacrificial suffering and death, along with his abiding presence with the believing community in the context of a simple meal. In the life of each believer it is a threefold mystery of banquet, presence, and sacrifice that puts him or her in close personal contact with person of Jesus Christ. This was true for the apostles at the Last Supper, for the disciples at Emmaus, for the early Christian community—and it is true today. The Eucharist lies at the heart of the gospel message. Like the disciples at Emmaus, Christians today still marvel at how he makes himself known to them in the breaking of the bread.

ON THE ROAD TO EMMAUS

- Do you view the Eucharist as banquet, presence, and sacrifice?
- Which of these do you find easiest to accept?
- Which do you find most difficult to understand?
- Do you believe that Jesus, the Risen Lord, reveals himself in the Eucharist?
- Do you believe that he reveals himself to you personally in the breaking of the bread?
- Why is the Eucharist so central to the Catholic faith?
- Do you consider the Eucharist central to your life?

MY BURNING HEART

Lord, help me to see with the eyes of faith. Help me to enter into the mystery of the Eucharist and to place it at the center of my life. Help me to receive this sacrament with reverence and awe at your real and vital presence in it. Through it, help me to immerse myself in your passion, death, and resurrection. Help me to recognize you in the breaking of the bread and to sense your presence in the community gathered there. Help me to become Eucharist for others.

CHAPTER SIX

CALLED *to* COMMUNITY

The Emmaus story is also about the call to community. It begins with the two disciples leaving Jerusalem with their hearts troubled over the recent events surrounding Jesus' passion and death and the discovery of the empty tomb. Although no one knows exactly why they were setting out on their own, it is possible that the physical movement away from Jerusalem carries with it a subtle spiritual and psychological displacement from the community of disciples that Jesus left behind. It is possible that they were leaving Jerusalem out of disillusionment over what had happened to their master and fear over what might happen to them if they were identified as his followers.

Whatever the case, once they recognize Jesus in the breaking of the bread, the attention of the two disciples turns toward Jerusalem and they set out immediately to share their experience of the Risen Lord with the group that had remained behind. This movement back toward Jerusalem represents the call to community that resonates within the heart of every disciple. Jesus entrusted his message to his disciples as a group, for he wanted them to live and work as one. Life in community was one of the distinctive features of the early Christian community. The return of the two disciples from Emmaus to Jerusalem represents an early recognition of this call, one that follows almost immediately upon the recognition of Jesus in the breaking of the bread.

A Spirituality of Communion

The word "community" means "being one with." In the Christian understanding, it is the visible expression of "communion," the state of "being one with God and one another." The time and effort put into "being one with" our brothers and sisters in Christ is often called "building community." Doing so is vital to our faith and essential to our identity as church. With it, even our most difficult challenges are easier to bear. Without it, even the simplest of tasks can become burdensome and difficult to face. Building community is essential to the proper functioning of the body of believers. Although everyone has a part to play, it ultimately comes to us through God's Spirit working in our hearts. By cooperating with these internal promptings, we are inspired to think and act in certain ways for the good of the believing community. Our role is not insignificant. We are the ones who allow the Spirit to work through us.

The phrase, or at least the idea, of "spirituality of communion" has appeared a number of times in recent magisterial documents.[33] Rooted in the Conciliar term *communio*, a rich theological concept with many nuances and which itself is rooted in the New Testament notion of fellowship (*koinonia*), the phrase has emerged in recent years as a paradigm of Catholic self-understanding that concerns both Catholic identity and mission.[34] The two obviously go hand in hand: it is impossible to be "faithful to God's plan" without attempting to respond in some way to the "world's deepest yearnings." A "spirituality of communion" involves both heart and mind. It concerns the heart's contemplation of "the mystery of the Trinity dwelling within us."[35] The Holy Trinity rests at the very pinnacle of the Catholic hierarchy of truths. Contemplating its presence within us reminds us of the sacredness of human life and the call to blessedness that we all share. It is because the Trinity dwells within us that we are able to see its light shining on our brothers and sisters around us. Because of the mutual indwelling that we share, we begin to think of ourselves as intimately tied up with the lives of those around us. Their joys and sorrows become our own; their needs, our needs. We consider them our friends and actively seek their well-being. We look to their various gifts and talents as blessings for the entire mystical body. We make room for them in our lives and bear their burdens. Most importantly, it moves us to resist and overcome those self-centered tendencies within us that involve us in "competition, careerism, distrust, and jealousy."[36]

A genuine "spirituality of communion" is rooted in the very life of the Trinity, which manifests itself inwardly in the life of the believer and then radiates outward toward our brothers and sisters in the faith and then toward other members of the human family. Without this inner contemplative dimension, which expresses itself in concrete actions of loving concern for others, the external structures of communion will not serve their purpose and become "'masks' of communion rather than its means of expression and growth." The "spirituality of communion," moreover, also has practical significance. It warns against premature and unreflective action that fails to promote authentic Christian values. It should be the guiding principle of all levels of Catholic formation, be it in the home, the school, the parish, the novitiate, the seminary, or the university. Wherever Christians are formed, this "spirituality of communion" should be the underlying principle that shapes their vision of the world and that ultimately spurs them to action. Actions that do not flow from this underlying spirit and way of life—even when done in the name of or for the good of the church—cannot be considered authentically "Catholic."[37]

Building Christian Community

Given the seriousness of the task, it is important that we have a clear idea of what exactly is being asked of us. Serious thought must be given to what building up the body of Christ, the church, actually entails. Here are some concrete suggestions that may be of some help.

....

Gathering Ourselves. We cannot build community without ever getting together. To deny this necessity would be to ignore the physical dimension of our lives and our very real need to give visible expression to our deepest hopes. We should not have to look for reasons to come together. All we need to do is to take advantage of the opportunities that come to us in our daily lives: going for a walk with a friend, having the neighbors over for a barbecue, going to a community function or a prayer meeting at the local church. Nothing could be more natural. Inviting others to join us in the normal activities of our lives tells them that they are important to us. It is hard to do so, however, if we are never physically together in the same room or outdoor space. A community needs to spend time together. The occasions can arise spontaneously or come about through forethought and careful planning. Organizers of such events should take special care not to exclude any members of the community.

....

Connecting. Building community, however, involves more than just getting people to be in the same place with each other. Connections need to be made. A community is more than just a group of individuals gathered together in the same space for a common event or purpose. For a community to take shape, people need to be given the opportunity to get to know one another. They need to recognize names and faces. They need to know something about each other's lives. Communities consist of a vast web of personal relationships that need to be nurtured and continually maintained. For this reason, it is important that people be able to have a certain degree of familiarity with those around them. That is not to say that all members of a community—be it a family, a church, a religious order or lay association—will be close friends, but only that they know and respect each other well enough to feel a certain amount of ease in each other's presence.

Sharing Our Experiences. One way of nurturing these relationships is by getting people to share their experiences with each other. We do this all the time with those we love. We tell them our story, and we allow them to tell us theirs. Doing so helps us to see life differently. Telling our story is a way of taking ownership of what happens to us. It forces us to choose a certain narrative sequence of events and to identify ourselves with it. Our image of ourselves is closely related to the stories we tell. When we allow someone to tell us their story, we are letting them know that we respect them and value what they have to say. When they allow us to tell them ours, they make us feel as though we belong and that our opinion really matters. If we do not share our experiences, we will never get to know one another and can easily end up dealing with others on the level of appearances or, worse still, from our unspoken prejudices.

....

Listening. If we tell our stories to each other, it is important that they be heard. In today's world, it is becoming increasingly difficult to find someone who truly knows how to listen. Many people think they are listening when, in reality, they are only quietly waiting for the next opportunity to speak. Many of us are experts at carrying on extensive monologues with those we meet. True listening involves an act of selflessness. It means being present to the person before us in such a way that all that really matters to us at that particular moment is trying to understand what is being said and the feelings behind it. Listening is essential for the art of conversation. It means hearing what is being said and reflecting it back in such a way that the other person understands that we understand. We are quickly losing touch with this important skill. Building community means teaching people how to listen and encouraging them to make this a priority in their dealing with others.

....

Pondering Life. Once we have learned to listen, we can begin to help one another to ponder the meaning of our lives. This involves looking at our lives with a special interest in discovering what God might be saying to us through the people we meet and the events that happen to us. It means casting a discerning eye to our hearts so that we will be able to understand what we truly value in life. It also entails looking to the Scriptures and to the tradition of the church to find valuable points of reference for interpreting our experience. Pondering our lives means being willing to delve beneath the surface of things and to take a good, hard look at what we find there. It asks us to dedicate ourselves to searching for our purpose in life and to finding adequate tools for interpreting our experiences. By pondering our lives, we come to a deeper understanding of ourselves, the world we live in, and the God who calls us out of darkness into life.

....

Growing Together. Pondering life opens up for us new avenues of growth. Building community means taking advantage of the insights we have gained through our common sharing, listening, and discernment. Doing so means that we often need to challenge others and to be challenged by them. As we grow together, we acquire a deeper sensitivity to the quiet rhythm of life within us. We become more aware of the various growing pains we ourselves have gone through and appreciate them all the more when we encounter them in others. Growth of any kind cannot be rushed. We must set our roots down before we sprout toward the sun and spread out our branches. As we mature over time, we learn to be patient with each other and remember the importance of keeping our eyes fixed on what we hope one day to become. We also are able to look back at our lives and remember what we were like at different periods of our lives. By growing together, we are able to help each other to see how we have changed over time and what areas of our lives still need attention.

Respecting Boundaries. Building community also means learning to respect the privacy of others. The goal of community is to generate a sense of belonging that will enable unique individuals to become a part of something greater than themselves. For this to happen, however, communities must be careful not to move without warrant into the private lives of their members. Care must be taken that the relationship between an individual and the community be nurtured on the basis of freedom and responsible service. Both individuals and communities, moreover, need to be sensitized to the ways in which they can take advantage of one another. For this to happen, time needs to be set aside within the community for honest discussion about how proper balance can be kept between individual needs and community demands. The level and intensity of such a discussion will depend on the type of community we are talking about (e.g., family, local parish, religious community) and the particular needs it wishes to address at any given time.

Serving One Another. Building community also means teaching community members how to serve the needs of others.

To do so, it is important that efforts be made to help people to identify genuine needs, to find practical ways in which those needs can be met, and then to take an active role in doing something about it. A spirit of generous service should lie at the heart of every Christian community. Such service should be directed within the community but also reach beyond it. Community members need to be careful of limiting their focus solely to their own immediate needs. As important as these are, it is essential for members to foster an outward-looking vision that moves them beyond their private interests and brings them face-to-face with the needs of the wider community. In doing so, they will begin to understand what it means to place the needs of others before their own and to act accordingly.

Celebrating Life. Building community means celebrating life. We celebrate life out of a deep sense of gratitude to God for the gifts we have received. Such thankfulness flows out of and is intimately bound up with divine worship. No true celebration can be devoid of the sense of the sacred. The more we perceive the presence of the divine in our lives, the more we are able to stand in awe of the wonder of existence. To celebrate life means to seek God in all things and to offer him praise, adoration, and thanksgiving both individually and as a community of believers. For a community of believers, one of the primary ways of celebrating life is through the church's sacramental worship. These outward signs of God's presence in our lives help us to probe the depths of Christ's life, death, and resurrection. Through them, we are drawn more deeply into the mystery of Christ and his church. As a result, we come to a better knowledge of ourselves, our vocation as Christians, and the world we are called to serve.

Engaging the World. This spirit of generous service should encourage people to look beyond themselves and to think of community as a vehicle enabling them to situate themselves, and to participate more fully, in the world around them. Building community means helping people to interpret the world around them and to find ways of responding that coincide with their shared vision of life. When seen in this light, community is not meant to be a retreat from the world but a viable way through which its members can actively engage it. A community does so by identifying issues needing to be addressed, evaluating the various factors involved, and formulating practical strategies for change that will enable it to act in a consistent and decisive way. By belonging to a community, people choose not to remain passive or indifferent onlookers in the world they live in; instead, they are empowered to play an active role in shaping it according to the Christian principles they profess.

These are some of the basic building blocks of Christian community. They are not the only ones, but they number among the most important. Setting them in place takes a long time and requires the help of many hands. They also need the constant support of prayer and our deep, personal devotion to Christ.

Conclusion

When the two disciples return to the community of disciples they had left behind in Jerusalem, they are blessed with a second experience of the Risen Lord, this time not in the breaking of the bread but in the midst of community. While they are sharing their experience with the eleven and their companions and hearing the news that the Lord has indeed appeared to Simon, Jesus himself stands in their midst and says, "Peace be with you." He shows them his hands and feet to calm their fears of seeing a ghost and invites them to touch his flesh and bones to see that he is truly risen from the dead. Since their reaction is a mixture of joy, wonder, and disbelief, he asks them for something to eat and consumes a piece of boiled fish to calm their fears still further (Luke 24:36–43).

Jesus then opens their minds to understand everything in the law of Moses, the prophets, and the psalms that referred to his passion, death, and resurrection. He instructs them to proclaim his message of repentance and the forgiveness of sins; he tells them that they are to be witnesses of all that has happened and that they are to stay in Jerusalem until they are clothed with power from on high. He then lifts up his hands, blesses them, and is carried up into heaven. Overwhelmed with joy, the disciples worship him and go into the temple continually to bless God. The story of Emmaus ends with an experience of the Risen Lord in the midst of the community of disciples. Along with the teaching of the apostles, the prayers, and the breaking of the bread, community life would become a hallmark of the early church (Luke 24:36–53; Acts 2:42). It remains so to this very day.

Since building community is everyone's responsibility, it is important for community members to have a good sense of what is expected of them and how to go about it. Taken together, the suggestions outlined in this chapter provide us with a firm foundation for rooting our lives in sound gospel values. Such values, however, need to be discovered anew by each generation of Christians and incorporated into the fabric of their daily lives. Building strong Christian communities is one of the best ways of making sure that this happens. Christians who do not dedicate themselves to this process deprive themselves of one of the most valuable supports available to them. Those who do, however, have chosen wisely and, like the two disciples at Emmaus, will find themselves well prepared for what they will one day discover at their journey's end.

ON THE ROAD TO EMMAUS

- With which local Christian community do you identify most?
- How do you contribute to it?
- What concrete efforts have you taken to build community there?
- What areas of building community do you need to work on?
- How does being part of a community challenge you?
- Do you promote a spirituality of communion in your relations with others?
- Are you walking away from Christian community or toward it?

MY BURNING HEART

Lord, help me to find my place in community. Help me to walk toward it, not away from it. Help me be patient with others, and also with myself. Help me to live in communion with others, to build community rather than tear it down. Help me to learn from others and allow others to learn from me. Help me to find my balance in the way I relate to my community. Teach me to sense your presence in the midst of my community. Help me to reach out to others, and help me to allow myself to be touched by them.

CONCLUSION

The story of the two disciples on the road to Emmaus resonated in the hearts of the early Christian community, for it spoke to their experience and enabled them to translate the events of Christ's passion, death, and resurrection to their present circumstances. The story functions in much the same way today, since we can see our own experience reflected in it, and it touches our hearts in a way that only Scripture can. The story reminds us that Jesus walks besides us in our journey of faith and wishes to reveal to us his true identity. For this to happen, however, we must first be willing to enter into conversation with him by revealing ourselves to him on the level of mind and heart.

The story reveals five essential traits of Christian discipleship, reminding us that we are called to be men and women of Prayer, Scripture, Friendship, Eucharist, and Community.

Prayer is one of the mainstays of the life of discipleship and must be taken seriously if we ever wish to reach our journey's end. In addition to prayer, Jesus also calls us to seek him in his word.

Scripture gives us more than mere knowledge about God; it also conveys an experience of him. God speaks to us through the words of Holy Writ, and we are called to listen for him in the silence of our hearts. Only then will he reveal himself and commune with us. Scripture enlightens the soul and enables us to sense the presence of the Lord both within our hearts and in our midst.

As he accompanies us on our way, Jesus slowly befriends us and asks us to do the same with those we meet. We too are called to befriend those we encounter in our journey of faith by sharing with them the fruits of our own intimate friendship with Christ. *Friendship* in Christ builds up the body of Christ.

We affirm this friendship whenever we gather around the table of the Lord for *Eucharist*. There, Jesus reveals himself to the eyes of faith, invites those present to share in his paschal mystery, and befriends anyone who delves beneath appearances in order to sense his presence in their midst.

Authentic Christian *community* flows from the celebration of the Eucharist and is one of the building blocks of God's kingdom. Like the early Christians, we are called to dedicate ourselves to the teaching of the apostles, life in community, the breaking of bread, and the prayers (Acts 2:42).

Like the two disciples, we too are called to encounter Jesus on the road. Like them, we too are called to be men and women of Prayer, Scripture, Friendship, Eucharist, and

Community. Like them, we too are called to have hearts burning with a desire for and a deep love for God and neighbor. Like them we are called to seek him in the breaking of the bread. These are the marks of true discipleship. Without them, our journey of faith will be all the more difficult and its outcome, at best, uncertain. With them, our minds and hearts will be focused on the power of God's love revealed to us in the passion, death, and resurrection of his Son, Our Lord Jesus Christ. This love is the one thing that matters. Such is the lesson of Emmaus. It is a lesson of discipleship that must be learned anew by every generation.

ENDNOTES

1. Throughout this work, all references to Scripture come from *Holy Bible: New Revised Standard Version with Apocrypha* (New York/Oxford: Oxford University Press, 1989).

2. See Raymond E. Brown, *An Introduction to the New Testament* (New York: Doubleday, 1997), 273-74.

3. Robert North and Philip J. King, "Biblical Archeology," in *The New Jerome Biblical Commentary*, eds. Raymond E. Brown, Joseph A. Fitzmyer, and Roland E. Murphy (Upper Saddle River, NJ: Prentice Hall, 1990), 1218 (no. 154). See also, Brown, *Introduction to the New Testament*, 261.

4. See Brown, *Introduction to the New Testament*, 279, 319-22.

5. See Dennis J. Billy, *Evangelical Kernels: A Theological Spirituality of the Religious Life* (Staten Island: Alba House, 1993), 171-72.

6. Ibid., 171.

7. Ibid., 170-71. For more on this tripartite anthropology and its impact on the Christian tradition, see Henri de Lubac, *Theology in History*, trans. Anne Englund Nash (San Francisco: Ignatius Press, 1996), 117-200.

8. These forms of prayer are briefly examined in Dennis J. Billy, "A Profound Form of Prayer," *Liguorian* 103 (no. 9, 2015): 10-15.

9. See *Catechism of the Catholic Church*, nos. 2700-2704.

10. Ibid., nos. 2705-8.

11. Ibid., nos. 2709-2719.

12. Ibid., nos. 1066-1075. For the relationship between liturgy and life, see Jean Corbon, *The Wellspring of Worship*, trans. Matthew J. O'Connell (San Francisco: Ignatius Press, 2005), 199-262.

13. Irenaeus of Lyons, *Adversus haereses*, 4.20.7.

14. Alphonsus de Liguori, *Prayer, The Great Means of Obtaining Salvation*, in *The Complete Works of Saint Alphonsus de Liguori*, ed. Eugene Grimm, vol. 3 (Brooklyn, St. Louis, Toronto: Redemptorist Fathers, 1927), 21.

15. Ibid., 49.

16. Ibid., 63.

17. Augustine of Hippo, *Sermon* 22:7.

18. See *Catechism of the Catholic Church*, nos. 115-17. For a detailed exposition of these senses, see Henri de Lubac, *Medieval Exegesis: The Four Senses of Scripture*, 3 vols. trans. Mark Sebanc (Grand Rapids, MI: Eerdmans, 1998-2009).

19. See *Catechism of the Catholic Church*, no. 118.

20. See John Cassian, *Conferences*, 2.14.8.

21. See C.S. Lewis: *The Four Loves* (San Diego/New York/London: Harvest, 1960), 91.

22. For a detailed analysis of these four loves, see Ibid., 53-192.

23. *Nicomachean Ethics*, 1156a7-1158b7.

24. Ibid., 1155b31-34, 1156a3-b12, 1170b5-10. The specific English terms come from Paul J. Wadell, *Friendship and the Moral Life* (Notre Dame, IN: University of Notre Dame Press, 1989), 130-31, 136-37.

25. Thomas Aquinas, *Summa theologiae*, II-II, q. 23, a. 1, resp.

26. Aelred of Rievaulx, *Spiritual Friendship*, trans. Mary Eugenia Laker, with an Introduction by Douglas Roy, Cistercian Series 5 (Kalamazoo, MI: Cistercian Publications, 1977), 103.

27. Ibid., 104-5, 127.

28. Second Vatican Council, *Lumen gentium* ("The Dogmatic Constitution on the Church"), no. 11. See also *Catechism of the Catholic Church*, no. 1324.

29. See Billy, *Evangelical Kernels*, 135-38.

30. Ibid., 139.

31. Ibid., 139-41.

32. Ibid., 142-43.

33. See, for example, John Paul II, *Novo millennio ineunte* ("Apostolic Letter on the New Millennium"), no. 43; Idem, V *ita consecrata* (Apostolic Exhortation on the Consecrated Life"), nos. 46-47. Note also the close relationship between *communio* and *missio* developed in Idem, *Christifideles laici* ("Apostolic Exhortation on the Laity"), nos. 31-32 and in Idem, *Pastores dabo vobis* ("Apostolic Exhortation on the Priesthood"), no. 12.

34. For the theological significance of *communio*, see Joseph Ratzinger, "Communio—a Program," *Communio* 19(1992): 443-49. For the Church as *communio*, see Avery Dulles, *Models of the Church* (Garden City, NY: Doubleday, 1974): 51-66.

35. See John Paul II, *Novo millennio ineunte*, no. 43.

36. Ibid.

37. Ibid.

I Want to See
*What the Story of Blind Bartimaeus Teaches Us
about Fear, Surrender, and Walking the Path to Joy*
ROC O'CONNOR, SJ

Theologian and famed composer Roc O'Connor invites us into the Gospel of Mark to sit by the side of the road with blind Bartimaeus. O'Connor shows us how Bartimaeus sits not only at the roadside but at the center of everything Mark wants us to know about being a disciple of Jesus. An insightful and prayerful book!

128 PAGES | $14.95 | 5½" X 8½" | 9781627853279

Holy Wind, Holy Fire
Finding Your Vibrant Spirit through Scripture
PAMELA A. SMITH, SS.C.M.

How can we get to know and draw closer to this Third Person of the Holy Trinity, who has the power to transform us and give us a share in the very life of God? Sister Pamela invites us into a wonderful journey through the Old and New Testaments to catch glimpses of the Spirit at work. Reading, reflecting, and praying with this book will help to re-energize and reawaken us to the energy and joy that only the Holy Spirit can give.

136 PAGES | $14.95 | 5½" X 8½" | 9781627853170

A Deep, Abiding Love
Pondering Life's Depth with Julian of Norwich
JENNIFER LYNN CHRIST

Jennifer Christ draws parallels between Julian's times and ours and demonstrates how Julian's message of hope and joy in God's never-ending love for us can give us strength and hope. Scholars have called Julian a theological optimist. Spend time with this book—reading Julian's words, praying with them, pondering, and journaling, and letting her hope-filled message take root in your heart.

128 PAGES | $14.95 | 5½" X 8½" | 9781627853156